PORT PERFORMANCE

PORT TANGIBLE AND INTANGIBLE RESOURCES IN ACHIEVING HIGHER PORT PERFORMANCE

SALWANI ARBAK | RABIUL ISLAM

Made with ♥ on the Notion Press Platform
www.notionpress.com

This research was supported by Research and Innovation Management Centre (RIMC), Universiti Utara Malaysia under Universiti Grant. We would like to express our deepest gratitude to the Vice Chancellor, Universiti Utara Malaysia UUM, Deputy Vice Chancellor (Research and Innovation), (UUM) and all staffs from Research and Innovation Management Centre & SOIS staffs of UUM specially Professor Dr. Mohamad Hanapi Mohamad and Assoc. Prof. Dr. Nik Ab. Halim Nik Abdullah for the time and guidance contributed towards the completion of this research project.

Contents

Preface

The main theme of this book is on port performance managers to deliver has reached a critical level, as policymakers, port users and other stakeholders, such as those involved in the environment and security, are compiling data directly and/or regulating performance reporting. If ports do not proactively participate in efforts to bench their performance, we expect that a number of stakeholders will do it for them. Modern management practices seek to link performance measurement to strategic planning processes in an increasingly competitive marketplace for port services. Competition itself can be understood as taking place among ports between port authorities, and among ports as well as within a port between operators. Port managers are required to measure and communicate achievements in this dynamic strategic environment.

The ultimate goal of strategic management research is to search for the explanation of why some firms are more successful than their competitors. This book applies the Resource-based View Theory to get a full understanding of how ports capitalize the resources and competency to compete and improve port performance. This study identifies factors that can increase the port's performance by analysing the relationship between port tangible and intangible resources and port performance. Port tangibles resources include financial assets, physical assets and technology assets, whereas port intangible assets include intellectual property assets, organizational assets and port capabilities. A total of 123 respondents from major ports in Malaysia were involved in this survey. This book found out that one dimension of port intangible resources which is port capabilities do have a significant influence on port performance. However, two other dimensions of intangible assets which are intellectual property assets and organizational assets have no significant influence on port performance. The findings of this study are expected to have implications for the port industry on the importance of port capabilities in improving port performance and competitiveness.

Acknowledgements

This research was supported by Research and Innovation Management Centre (RIMC), Universiti Utara Malaysia under Universiti Grant. We would like to express our deepest gratitude to the Vice Chancellor, Universiti Utara Malaysia UUM, Deputy Vice Chancellor (Research and Innovation), (UUM) and all staffs from Research and Innovation Management Centre & SOIS staffs of UUM specially Professor Dr. Mohamad Hanapi Mohamad and Assoc. Prof. Dr. Nik Ab. Halim Nik Abdullah for the time and guidance contributed towards the completion of this research project.

CHAPTER ONE: INTRODUCTION OF PORT PERFORMANCE

CHAPTER ONE: INTRODUCTION OF PORT PERFORMANCE

1. **Background of study**

The tremendous growth of the Malaysian port industry over the last few years underlines the value of the maritime economic sector to its economic well-being. The ports are recognized as essential contributors in facilitating trade, hence crucial to its economic prosperity. Ports are also acting as gateways to domestic and international trade. Connecting the region as well as the intra-region to the world is crucial in global logistical network{Winkelmans, 2002 #562;Chang, 2007 #566}. The crucial importance of the port industry to the country's economic prosperity can be seen by the commitment of the Malaysian government to invest in the sector as demonstrated in the Regional Economic Corridor. The Business Times of 27 August2013 reported that the Malaysian government had spent RM1 billion to upgrade the external infrastructure to support the expansion of the Port of Kuantan (Rupa, 2013). This shows that the Malaysian government really makes an effort to improve the competitiveness and performance of the Malaysian ports.

The phenomenal growth in global trade and the current trends in the logistic industry has had a huge impact in the competition of the port industry.Dong-Wook and Panayides (2012) argued that the port industry is substantially changing due to a number of factors, namely changes in the market environment, globalisation, transport revolution, logistic integration and the consequent expansion of the maritime industry. Among other external factors are the continuing growth in container traffic, increases in ship size, consolidation of port operators with global terminal operators, and increases in port infrastructure investment.

According to Ducruet and Notteboom (2012), the introduction of the containerization acted as a catalyst for world trade growth. In 2011, global container trade was estimated at 151 million TEUs (twenty foot equivalent unit), a 7 percent increase over 2010 (UNCTAD, 2012). This shows the increasing demand for maritime transport as it is a rising method to transport and exchange goods all over the world.

The continuous demand for containerization and sea transportation has been spurred by the emergence of mega vessels owned by global carriers. In early 2012, twenty leading operators accounted for about 70 percent of the total container capacity deployed. The three largest companies were based in Europe, while six of the remaining top 10 were based in Asia (Vincent & Hassiba, 2013). On February 13 2013, the latest mega vessel called as Maersk Triple-E with 18,000 TEU capacity owned by Mearsk Line, was launched in Korea. Triple-E class vessels will revolve around the main ports in China, South East Asia, and Europe. Maersk Line believes that demand on the Asia– Europe trade will increase 5-8 per cent per year during 2011 to 2015 (Maersk, 2011). In the same period and it was forecasted that there would be 200 container fleets with similar capacity sailing from port to port around the world(Miller, 2009).

The growth of containerisation and the increasing size and capacity of vessels have changed the landscape of the portand shipping industries(Notteboom & Rodrique, 2011). The shipping companies particularly liners have to cover wider geographical areas to provide a wider range of services to meet the increasing diversified demand pattern of lower price and higher quality than before. In order to deal with these requirements, shipping companies have integrated horizontally through mergers, acquisitions and strategic alliances, and vertically through operating dedicated terminals (Notteboom, 2004) with competitive ports around the world. The new landscape requires port operators and port authorities to continuously access the availability of port resources and capabilities in order to meet the demand of their partners and stay competitive in the market. Besides that ports also have to make huge investments to provide better port infrastructure, efficient services, deep water, wide channel and , longer berths, suitable high speed cargo-handling equipment, suitable berths for coastal feeder vessels and goods road and rail intermodal connections to inland destination (Ircha, 2001). By having these resources and capabilities, they would be able to attract more volume of cargoes from their clients, thus leading to high performance, reduced maritime transport costs, avoidance of port congestion and ship waiting time and allowing ships to achieve economies of scale as well as high levels of productivity and efficiency (Tongzon, 2007).

The best example is the Port of Hong Kong, which possesses an excellent combination of resources and capabilities such as good intermodal infrastructure with 285 hectares of land, providing 24 berths and 8,530 metres deep-water frontage. Moreover, its terminal has a water depth of 15.5 metres and with these capacities this port is able to handle over 22 million TEUs per year (Lun, Lai, & Cheng, 2009, p. 139).

Looking at the current trends and the competitive scenarios, an understanding of the anatomy of competitive advantage is of paramount importance to general managers who bear the ultimate responsibility for a firm's long-term survival and success. Barney (1991) argued that a competitive firm should have the ability to implement and conceive its strategies by making use of its resources, assets, capabilities, organisational process, firm's attributes, information and knowledge to achieve competitive advantage. In such situations, port authorities and port operators whose objectives are significantly economic are forced to re-assess their roles and identify their specific competencies that would enable them to achieve and sustain competitive advantage (Yang, Low, & Tang, 2011). In other words, ports need to recognise and capture new opportunities, define the new core business, as well as specify relevant core and threshold competencies in order to overcome the above-mentioned challenges and to stay ahead of competitors (Hamel & Prahalad, 1994).

However, to achieve these objectives ports are required to continually assess their performance relative to the rest of the world so that appropriate strategies can be devised to meet the challenges and increased demand (Tang, Low, & Lam, 2011).Collis (1991) argued that firm strategy is constrained by and dependent on the firm's resource profile. In order to improve port performance, it is crucial for port managers to know how to manage and make efficient use of its resources. This requires capabilities to manage its resources as the role of resource management depends on the contribution of the managerial actions. Simon et al., (2008) highlighted that the firm would achieve competitive advantage if the management could affectively bundle and deploy the organization's resources. They stated that the role of resource management is to focus on the contribution of the managerial the actions in managing the firm's resources. Thus, managerial action is important in understanding how competitive advantage is created and sustained. They added that the experience of the management will affect the productive services that all the organization's other resources are capable of. The influence of managerial experience is manifested through the process of resource management (Penrose, 1959).

The importance of resource management in the context of the port industry has been highlighted by Gordon et al. (2005) who agreed port competitiveness is dependent on the combination of the resources allocation by its management team. They added that the critical success factor of the Port of Singapore Authority (PSA)is not only being able to exploit and develop its natural resources but also able being to develop its skills and capabilities of its tangible and intangible resources.

Various schools of thought have been discussed in previous studies on the main factors of port competitiveness and performance. Ports have traditionally made use of quantitative measures to assess their performance. Mentzer and Konrad (1991) define performance as an investigation of effectiveness and efficiency in the accomplishment of a given activity and where the assessment is carried out in relation to how well the objectives have been met. To achieve this objective, economic activities have to make use of the so-called performance measures or indicators. However, measuring performance is not easy because there are many performance dimensions that cannot be captured particularly the extent to which customers are satisfied.

Previous port studies show that port efficiency is among the popular methods to measure port performance (Martinez-Budria et al., 1999; Cotto and Millan et al., 2000; Chen, 1998; Tongzon, 1995; Drewry, 2002; Tongzon and Ganesalingam, 1994; Coto and Millan, 2000; Park and De, 2004, Barros and Anthanasiou, 2004; Cullinane and Song, 2003). In the studies, the scholars are more focused on the efficiency of the terminal and berthing facilities. This is because the optimization of the terminal is important to ensure that the port has higher productivity.

However, the trends in contemporary logistics and the emergence of the new economy show that successful ports can no longer sustain this approach. Besides efficiency, port effectiveness is another important measure for port performance. Magala (2004) argued that in order to achieve higher port performance ports should not only be efficient but also effective. He added that port effectiveness is determined by how much ports could capture the volume of cargoes and also can meet the demand and the needs of the clients by utilizing their resources and port capabilities. Port effectiveness also means that ports are able to meet the demands and the needs of their client within the supply chain. Thus in order to achieve these objectives, the roles of resource management is more than just to increase financial and operating performance but also covers the whole aspect of internal and external factors which is more dynamic and comprehensive.

1.2 Challenges of Port Performance

Firm resources are crucially important to sustain competitive advantage and enhance performance. To be successful, a firm must have the appropriate resources for the survival of a firm. Those resources also must be managed effectively to achieve competitive advantage (Barney and Arikan, 2001; Sirmon, Hitt and Ireland, 2007). This study highlights the ability of the port management to manage the resources that could lead to increase port performance.

Although the relationship between port resources and performance is significant, the role of intangible resources as an important determinant has been given less emphasised in port research. This situation is due to several factors. First, most of the scholars emphasized the external industry factors as the principal sources of competitive advantage and port performance (Langen, 2002; Langen & Pallis, 2007; Musso, Ferrari, & Benacchio, 2001; Olivier, 2005; A. A. Pallis, Notteboom, & Langen, 2008). This idea was drawn from the New Industrial Organisation School of Thought. Among the important contributions is the application of the concept of entry barriers, monopoly power, vertical and horizontal integration, strategic group, port cluster, merger and consolidation to enhance port performance and competitiveness.

Second, based on previous port studies, the widely accepted approach was measuring port performance based on port efficiency. Port efficiency is measured by the efficiency of its inputs over its outputs. This method measures port performance through the analysis of data such as land area, employment (input) and throughput (output) (Martinez-Budria et al., 1999 and Coto-Millan et al, 2000, capital (input) and labour productivity (output) (Tongzon and Gunasingalam,1994), speed of container handling and vessel turnaround time (Peter, 2001). This stream of research takes port terminal as an area of study, where terminal, labour and vessel productivity are addressed.

However, the competitive advantage of a port is not only in providing efficient services at the terminal and in cargo handling but also in its ability to withstand the current trend and market, as well as its ability to upgrade and enhance resources and capabilities and find the most efficient way to satisfy customers' needs (Magala, 2004). Alternatively, the Resource-Based View (RBV) offers a new paradigm for ports to gain competitive advantage and enhance port performance. RBV of the firms predicts that certain types of resources owned and controlled by the firms have the potential and promise to generate competitive advantage which eventually leads to superior firm performance (Barney, 1991; Dierickx & Cool, 1989; Peteraf, 1993; Wernerfelt, 1984). The relationship between firm's resources and competitive advantage is significantly enhanced by the attributes and elements such as value, rareness, inimitable and non-substitutable (VRIN). Recently a study on resource attributes and performance in international joint ventures in Malaysia was conducted by Ainuddin, Beamish, Hulland, and Rouse (2007) which strengthens the significance of the VRIN of a firm. Peteraf (1993) has illustrated the fundamentals of the resource-based view in explaining competitive advantage by integrating firm's resources that would result in higher port performance. The study argues that resources must exhibit elements such as resource heterogeneity, imperfect mobility, ex-post and ex-ante limits to competition (imperfect imitability and imperfect substitutability) in order to significantly attain and sustain competitive advantage and eventually achieve superior firm performance.

A look at the different schools of thought contributing to port competitiveness raises one big question, which is addressed in this study. The question is: What are the most important factors that influence port competitiveness that lead to higher port performance? A review of extant port literature indicates that many factors act as major sources of competitive advantage. In general, with respect to port resources, the factors, which influence port competitiveness, can be split into two major categories, namely tangible and intangible resources. Previous studies on port competitiveness indicate that scholars tend to give more attention to port intangible resources, also referred to as port resources and capabilities. Among the critical factors are cultural differences (Luo, Van Hoek, & Roos, 2001), port reputation (Wiegmans, Hoest, & Notteboom, 2008), port management (Lirn, Thanopoulou, Beynon, & Beresford, 2004), service level (Peteraf, 1993), image marketing (Rozenblat, 2004), port ownership structure (Notteboom, Pallis, & Farrell, 2012), availability of skilled employees, quality of logistic services (Feng, Mangan, & Lalwani, 2012), quality management practice (Cheng & Choy, 2013) port cooperative relationship (Low & Tang, 2012) horizontal and vertical integration and concentric diversification (Parola, Satta, & Caschili, 2013).

Even though many scholars agreed that ports achieve competitive advantage from their unique combination of port resources and capabilities, scholars have differing views on what the main factors that could boost port competitiveness are. This raises the need to conduct an empirical study that examines the effect of port resources and capabilities on port competitiveness among Malaysian ports based on the Resource-Based View (RBV). The RBV perspective concentrates on what are known as port intangible resources components such as port structure, port control system, compensation policies, contractual agreement, reputation, culture, human resources management policies) and port dynamic capabilities (e.g. relation ability, routines, employees and managers know-how). Other than these components, tangible resources components (e.g., port strategic location, port financial capabilities and IT capabilities and port infrastructure) were also evaluated.

For this study, the RBV framework was used as a framework to analyse how Malaysian ports compete, and to identify the major factors that contribute to port competitiveness. Findings of previous studies have provide inadequate useful finding to be used as a guideline by practitioners to understand the complexity of resources and capabilities to increase port performance, as well as to formulate the right action plan in order to enhance port performance in the era of the borderless world. Therefore, it motivates the researcher to further uncover the nature of this issue.

1.3 Significance of Port Performance

The results of the research are expected to contribute to the theoretical, methodological and practical uses of the factors that contribute to the port performance in port industry in Malaysia.

From the theoretical perspective, the contributions of the present study are as follows:

i) This research verifies the RBV theory as its developed and conceptualized a system of port resources using the RBV framework. Most of the previous studies on port competitiveness tended to focus more on specific resources rather than the bundle or system of resources. Thus, this research indicates which analyses the influence of port resources and capabilities on port competitiveness among the major ports in Malaysia provides a new measurement and conceptualization especially to the RBV theory. As previous studies were more focused on different industries, the conceptual framework used in this research provides a strong foundation for the further research especially in the context of the port industry.

ii) Previous researchers highlighted those empirical studies on the understanding the influence of port resources and capabilities on port performance was lacking in the context of the Resource-Based View. In recognition of the need to bridge these gaps in knowledge pertaining to port performance, this study contributes to the body of literature by responding to the need for empirical research on the factors that influence port performance, and to validate the previous findings by applying the RBV framework. Despite there being many interesting studies on the influence of the port performance, they do not empirically address the critical issue of the influence of port intangible resources and capabilities on port performance. The empirical research on RBV is important and no single researcher or research study has defined the relationship fully (Levitas and Chi, 2002). Instead, different scholars have studied different aspects of connection. The boundaries between the concept of resources, skills and capabilities are not clear (Andersen and Suat Kheam, 1998). A better understanding of the influence of port the intangible resources and capabilities in port industry should give a clearer theoretical perspective on the nature that affects port performance using RBV framework, especially in the Malaysian port industry where the issue of port performance is becoming a major issue for a port's survival.

From the methodological perspective, the contribution of the present study is as follows:

Most popular methods of study of port performance and competitiveness are surveys (Lirn et al., 2004; Song & Yeo, 2004), analyses of port efficiency and productivity based on the data on ports(Barros & Athanassiou, 2004; Cullinane, Song, Ji, & Wang, 2004; Tongzon & Heng, 2005) and through 'formal' modelling(Lam & Yap, 2006; Magala & Sammons, 2008; Malchow & Kanafani, 2001). These methods have all added to the understanding of port performance and competitiveness. However, these methods have their own limitations, as for future research, data availability limits the analysis of port efficiency and performance, while port surveys may not yield detailed additional insight to the existing body of knowledge(Athanasios A Pallis, Vitsounis, & De Langen, 2010).

With regard to survey-based research, among the most influential methods to access port performance and competitiveness are the analytical hierarchy process approach (AHP), discrete choice analysis, input-oriented, outcome-oriented and process oriented models. However, most of these surveys were done in Western Europe, America and China. There are only a few studies on port performance using the survey-based method applying the Resource-Based Model(Gordon, Lee, & Lucas, 2005; Magala, 2004).In order to bridge the gap, this study will assess the influence of port resources and capabilities on port performance and test among major Malaysian ports using the Resource-Based View Model. The survey-based study using the RBV model is more robust as in term of the size and the samples of the study. Thus, this method is able to produce more reliable research findings.

For the practical perspective, the contributions of the present study are as follows:

The results of this research are expected to contribute to the body of knowledge specifically in the enhancement the of Resource-Based View framework within the context the of port industry. Identifying the influence of the port resources and capabilities on port performance will enable ports to formulate the best strategy based on their own resources and capabilities; therefore, it would enable the achievement of competitive advantage. As many ports are facing significant increases of demand in shipping, they need to integrate the best resources and capabilities to compete with their rivals. Knowing port core competencies and capabilities is very crucial not only for the achievement of a competitive advantage but also for port development, growth, and survival (Magala, 2004).

The findings of this study are important to enhance the performance and competitiveness of the Malaysian ports. As competition among the ports to attract shipping lines and handle more cargoes heats up, Malaysian ports must strive to leverage on their strengths and continuously improve their competency and provide value-added services to compete with neighbouring ports.

As the performance of the Malaysian ports are determined by various competitive factors such as location, highly skilled workers, port service, hinterland condition, convenience, logistics cost, regional centre and connectivity (Yeo, Roe, & Dinwoodie, 2008), the port industry in Malaysia is economically important and has shown marked improvement in its performance in recent years("Economic Performance and Prospects," 2014). Consequently, evaluating the performance and competitiveness of the port industry will improve the overall performance and competency.

1.4 Port Performance Approach

Research method is one of the important elements in research because it determines how the data will be collected and analysed. Thus, identifying the best research framework is very crucial for the researcher. This chapter will detail out the research design for each phase, sample and population of study, followed by procedures used when developing the survey questionnaire and during the data collection process. This chapter concludes with a description of the technique of analysis and statistical methods used at the empirical stage.

1. Approach and Justification of Port Performance

Research methods are selected based on the purpose and nature of the research. This research has both descriptive and explanatory elements. According to Sekaran and Bougie (2010), a descriptive research is conducted in order to describe the features of the variables of interest in a situation and portray the profile of situation. They claim that a deductive approach is appropriate for descriptive research to address the comparison. Second, this research is explanatory, as it explains the relationships between variables. Saunders, Lewis, and Thornhill (2009) noted that an explanatory study is used to establish relationships between variables and both deductive and inductive approach can be applied.

The primary objective of this study is to examine the relationship between port tangible assets, intangible assets and port performance. These objectives will be achieved through testing a series of theoretically justified research hypothesis. This study used the quantitative data collection approaches to test the posited hypotheses. According to Creswell (2008), there are three factors that influenced the selection of research methodology or design and these include research problems, researcher's personal experience and the target audience. In addition, Devers and Frankel (2000) added that, the other factors include research topic, type of population, sampling frame, characteristic of the sampling, type of research questions, response rate, budget, facilities provided, time frame for data collection and computer usage in data collection. In the selection of research method in this study, the researcher has considered some of the factors that and these include; target population, unit of analysis, the time constraint starting from the preparation until the completion of the thesis, availability of the sources and facilities during the data collection.

According to Punch (2003), the essence of quantitative research is the study of relationships between variables. He added, for the quantitative researcher, reality is conceptualized as variables, which are measured, and the primary objectives are to find how the variables are distributed and related to each other and why. Both the primary and secondary data were collected to facilitate hypothesis testing. Self-administered and mail survey questionnaire were used in order to obtain the primary data. A structured survey questionnaire was developed as it has the advantage to facilitative the collection of information in a systematic and orderly manner as the questions have been formulated in advance (Crisp, 1957). It is also can reach more geographically dispersed samples, more convenient and low in cost (Zikmund, 1991).

The second instrument is based on the secondary data. It is used to support the primary data and the sources are from the literature review and all other related documents such as port annual reports, newspaper, books and magazine and online journal. Further detail on the collection of secondary data will be explained in the next sub-chapter.

1. Population and Sample

The population for this study comprises all 15 major port operators in Malaysia. Of these 15 ports, 12 are Federal Ports which comprise of Port Klang (Westport and Northport), Penang Port, Johor Port, Port of Tanjung Pelepas, Kuantan Port, Kemaman Port, Miri Port, Rajang Port, Kuching Port, Sepangar Bay Port, Sabah Ports (include Kudat Port, Sandakan, Kunak and Tawau Port). The remaining three ports are Private State Port, which comprise ofPort Dickson and Labuan Port and Bintulu Port. The list of these ports is exhibited as Table 1.1.

No.

Population

Federal Ports

Participating Port
(Federal Ports)
Participating Port
(Federal Ports)
1.
Westport (M'sia) Sdn. Bhd.
1.Westport (Msia) Sdn. Bhd.
Western Region
2.
Northport (M'sia) Sdn. Bhd.
2. Northport (M'sia) Port Sdn. Bhd
Western Region
3.
Penang Port Sdn. Bhd.
3. Penang Port Sdn. Bhd
Northern Region
4.
Johor Port Bhd.

1. Johor Port Bhd.

Southern Region
5.
Port of Tanjung Pelepas Sdn. Bhd.

4. Port of Tanjung Pelepas Sdn. Bhd.

Southern Region
6.
Kuantan Port Consortium Sdn. Bhd.

5. Kuantan Port Consortium Sdn. Bhd.

Eastern Region
7.
Kemaman Port Sdn. Bhd.
8.
Miri Port
9.
Kuching Port
10
Sepangar Bay Port
11.
Rajang Port
12.
Sabah Port Sdn. Bhd.
Private State Ports
13.

14.
Bintulu Port Sdn. Bhd.
Port of Port Dickson

8. 7. Sabah Port Sdn. Bhd.
9. 8. Bintulu Port Sdn. Bhd.

10. East Malaysia
11. East Malaysia

15.
Port of Labuan
Table 1.1: Population and Sample of the Study
No.
Population
Federal Ports
Participating Port
(Federal Ports)
Participating Port
(Federal Ports)
1.
Westport (M'sia) Sdn. Bhd.
1.Westport (Msia) Sdn. Bhd.
Western Region
2.
Northport (M'sia) Sdn. Bhd.
2. Northport (M'sia) Port Sdn. Bhd
Western Region
3.
Penang Port Sdn. Bhd.
3. Penang Port Sdn. Bhd
Northern Region
4.
Johor Port Bhd.

3. Johor Port Bhd.

Southern Region
5.
Port of Tanjung Pelepas Sdn. Bhd.

4. Port of Tanjung Pelepas Sdn. Bhd.

Southern Region
6.
Kuantan Port Consortium Sdn. Bhd.

5. Kuantan Port Consortium Sdn. Bhd.

Eastern Region
7.
Kemaman Port Sdn. Bhd.
8.
Miri Port
9.
Kuching Port
10
Sepangar Bay Port
11.
Rajang Port
12.
Sabah Port Sdn. Bhd.
Private State Ports
13.
14.
Bintulu Port Sdn. Bhd.
Port of Port Dickson

8. 7. Sabah Port Sdn. Bhd.
9. 8. Bintulu Port Sdn. Bhd.

10. East Malaysia
11. East Malaysia

15.
Port of Labuan
Source: Malaysia Ministry of Transport

Of the 15 major ports operators in Malaysia, only eight ports were selected as the sample for this study. The sampling method for this study is cluster sampling. Refer to Table 1.1, all participating federal ports are the major ports in the West Malaysia, whereas the two participating private state port are the major ports in East Malaysia.

In term of regionalization, all participating ports in this study are divided into five major regions. For region that has more than two ports, two random samples were selected. The participating ports are namely: Kuantan Port Consortium Sdn. Bhd. from The Eastern Region, Northport (M'sia) Bhd. and Westport Malaysia Sdn. Bhd. from the Western Region, Port of Tanjung Pelepas and Johor Port Bhd. from the Southern Region, Penang Port Sdn. Bhd. from the Northern Region, Bintulu Port Sdn. Bhd. and Sabah Ports Sdn. Bhd. from the East Malaysia.

The unit of analysis of this study was the middle-level and top-level managers of the ports. The respondents for this study were selected based on few considerations. The key consideration was that they hold senior management positions within their organizations. Seniority was regarded as an important criterion because it is related to strategic decisions of a firm (Khatri & Ng, 2000). According to Rousseau (1985), organizational concepts should be measured at organizational level. Furthermore, Phillips (1981) stressed that the respondents or informants must have an adequate knowledge to answer the questionnaires in survey-type research and the authority of the potential informant should be considered in order to enhance the response rates.

The middle-level management consisted of departmental head, branch managers and senior executives. The top-level management consisted of the Board Directors and the Chief Executive Officer (include General Manager and Managing Director). Given that there are a limited number of respondents from the group of top and middle level management, a strategy to maximize the sample was to target at least 20 respondents including managers and senior executives from each port operator. This approach is accepted in the literature not only as a means of maximizing the number of respondents but also as a means of checking the consistency of responses within an organization (Khatri & Ng, 2000).

1.4.3 TEUs, numbers trade volumes and port profitability

Section A, which was on the demographic profile, asked the respondents to provide their personal and company information such as name of company, name of department, years of experience and education background. Section B asked about the impact of tangible and intangible resources on port performance. Lastly, section C, which is about the respondent's perception on port performance, which was measured by port profitability, number of TEUs, and total number of trade volume for the last three years.

Items that measure the independent and dependent variables used five-point Likert scale with available choices ranging from (1)-strongly disagree, (2)-disagree, (3)-neither agree nor disagree, (4)- agree, and (5)-strongly agree. It assigns an important weight to each dimension of the survey for each of the sections.

According to Das and Deng (2000), the difficulty in measuring many unobservable resources constructs, namely intangible resources, make it hard to use and assess secondary data with sufficient validity. Thus, one of the alternative approaches is to use a questionnaire. The structured questionnaire is designed as an alternative means of capturing data of unobservable resources construct. According to Hague (1993) a questionnaire is used based on four purposes. The first purpose is to draw accurate information from the respondents. The second purpose is to provide a structure to the interviewer so that it flows smoothly and orderly. The third purpose is to provide a standard format on which facts, comments and attitudes can be recorded. Finally, a questionnaire facilitates data processing.

1.4.4 Item Generation

To develop items for the resource constructs, a multiple-stage approach has been used as described by Dilman (1978). In order to develop scale items that best capture the domain of each construct, items from other instruments namely: Fahy (2002); Spanos and Lioukas (2001); Bank (2003); Gordon et al. (2005); Schroeder et al. (2002), Talley (2009), Ding (2009a); Welbourne and Wright (1997) are reviewed. The use of existing questionnaires saved time and reduced the work needed in developing a new questionnaire. It also carries some evidence of reliability and validity with it (Morgan & Hunt, 1994).

In order to select the items, item reliability was first checked to ensure that it meets the minimum acceptable thresholds (e.g., Cronbach alpha of 0.60 or greater). Second, both convergent and discriminate validity were examined to determine if the resources items predicted to measure a particular construct. Lastly, after all the items were generated, theoretical guidance and judgment was used to select the items that best meet the domain of the specific construct as defined in this study. However, the scales encapsulated items that were used in previous studies to maintain consistency.

1.4.5 Independent variables

Since the theoretical framework of this study is based on the Resource-Based View, the focus is on the exploitation of the port resources in order to gain a sustainable competitive advantage that affords the accrual superior performance. The next section will describe the items used to operationalize each construct. This includes the explanation of the independent variables, which consist of tangible and intangible resources.

In general, tangible resources consist of those resources that can be observed, are financial in nature, have physical properties, are owned and controlled by a firm, and are recorded on the firm's financial statement. According to Short (1993), tangible assets are categorized into financial and physical assets.

For the physical properties, they can generally be any asset that can be touched or seen, which are captured in the firm's financial statement, and are represented by an accounting-based monetary value. According to Vause (2009) physical assets are generally described as fixed assets held for use in the production or supply of goods and services. Meanwhile, as for the port related studies, physical assets included natural features, man-made features, infrastructure, superstructure and technology (Bank, 2003).

For this study, tangible resources consist of a variety of factors comprising of both financial and physical properties and port technological assets. Financial-based factors generally represent the firm's current assets and can be in a form of cash or assets that are capable of being converted to cash (Vause, 2001). The operationalization of financial assets construct consists of three main items that include cash on hand or at bank earned from operation, raised financial capital and financial investment.

Meanwhile, the operationalization of the physical assets construct consist of nine items, which included the building or tangible structure, the natural features, the hinterland and its location, the infrastructure & superstructure and port handling equipment. For port technology assets, the items are consist of port operational system, port Electronic Data Interchange, port integrated information system and port exit and entry control system.

For the intangible resources, based from the characteristic this resources that are hard to observe and are largely non-codifiable (Reed & DeFillippi, 1990), thus making it difficult to measure them. However, following the theoretical and conceptual standard are adapted from Welbourne and Wright (1997) and Grant (2002); Grant (202); Michalisin et al. (1997); Williamson (1985) and Barney (1991).Intangible resources are consists of four constructs: 1) intellectual property assets construct; 2) organizational assets construct; 3) reputational assets constructs; and 4) capabilities.

Intellectual property asset includes those resources that have a proprietary embodiment and can therefore, be protected by law. The operationalization of the intellectual property assets construct consists of five items that capture various characteristics of ideas, brands, invention and technology.

Organizational assets contribute order, stability, and quality to the firm. They provide a mechanism for exploiting a new market and revenue opportunities. The organizational assets construct was operationalized using four items that capture the characteristics of expanding or creating new market opportunities, facilitating a positive environment for achieving goals and objectives, acquiring, developing, retaining the human talent of the firm, and providing an efficient structure for day-to-day operations.

Reputational assets are the result of prior management actions. Reputational assets largely reflect the extent to which the firm is held in high esteem or regard. This construct is operationalized using four items that focus on different dimensions of firm's reputation including brand, product/services, customer services, and overall company reputation.

Finally, capability consists of the know-how that underlies a firm's ability to choose, develop, implement, and realize value-creating market strategies. The operationalization of capabilities consists of seven items that capture the dimensions of employee and managerial know-how based on the primary and secondary activities. The skills and managerial know-how are based on their intellectual, communication, planning and organizational skills, and the relationships with their external constituents, and the routine, which means the regular pattern of coordinated activities between individuals and teams.

1.4.6 Dependent Variables

Port performance is the dependent variable in this study. However, to measure port performance, this study use port performance as a measurement as it is usually used in the previous studies. Port performance are basically taken from the perspective of multiport performance evaluation (Talley, 2009). Port performance was operationalized using three measurement namely: port throughput volume, total number of TEUs loaded and unloaded and port profitability. Port profitability was operationalized by adapting a scale from Spanos and Lioukas (2001) which is based on port financial measurement.

Table 1.2: Financial assets scale

Scale Item/variables

Tangible Resources

Sources from previous research

Item 1: Cash (on hand/at bank) earned from port operations.

Hofer and Schendel (1978)

Item 2: Raised financial capital (e.g., debt from secured bank loans or equity from the issuance of share or bonds) at the last financial year.

Hofer and Schendel (1978)

Item 3: Financial investment (e.g., company shares in equity position in other companies).

Hofer and Schendel (1978)

Item 4: Port investment for the purpose of building physical assets that used in provision of port services (e.g. port way access, waterway and highway).

World Bank (2003)

In summary, the following tables provide a list of items for each different variable and most importantly the sources where these items were taken. Table 1.2, 1.3, 1.4 shows the items for tangible resources, while Table 1.5, 1.6, 1.7 shows the items for intangible resources while Table 1.8 shows the dependent variables.

Table 1.3: Physical Assets Scale

Scale Item/variables

Sources from previous research

Item 5: Building and other physical structure (e.g., offices, warehouse, terminal) including their location.

Hofer and Schendel (1978)

Item 6: Natural features (hydrographical data of region, availability of resources to build the port, tides and waves, weather and wind condition, hours of sunshine, rain level, natural harbour and land availability.

World Bank (2003)

Item 7: Port hinterland and port strategic location.

World Bank(2003)

Item 8: Port Infrastructure (port entrance, maritime assess channel, port inland transport such as road, tunnel and rail connection).

World Bank (2003)

Item 9: Port Equipment(e.g., dredging equipment cargo handling equipment, ship handling equipment and tugs).

World Bank (2003)

Item 10: Port support services (including the Free Trade/Industrial Zone, distribution and logistics centre).

New Item

Item 11: Ancillary services (e.g., pilotage, towage, ship repair at dockyard, security and fire-rescue).

New Item

Table 1.4: Technological Assets Scale

Item 12: Port Operational System (e.g., Computer Integrated Operational System, CITOS) to facilitate the berthing, handling of cargo and storage facilities).

Gordon et al.,(2005)

Item 13: Information Technology (Data Electronic Interchange, EDI or Trade net) which facilitate the processing of trade document and link with custom, shipping agents, ports, freight forwarders, traders etc.

World Bank (2003)

Item 14: Integrated information system (e.g., application of geographical information system (GIS), yard planning system, and port safety management system.

World Bank (2003)

Item 15: Exit and entry control system, track and trace of container, smart card at the entry and exit gate.

World Bank (2003)

Table 1.5: Intellectual Property Assets Scale

Scale Item/variables

Intangible Resources (Assets)

Sources from previous research

Item 16: Legally protected patent (an exclusive, legally- protected right which granted by the state to its inventor in respect of useful, new and inventive products and process).

Brooking (1996)

Item 17: Legally protected trademark (e.g., registered legally protected service or registered legally protected corporate brand).

Hall (1992)

Item 18: Proprietary/held-in-secret – all forms of held-in secret information, manufacturing, or other technology including software) specifically designed and/or developed to a firm's particular business model (PELCON III and CITOS).

Hall (1992)

Table 1.6: Organizational Assets Scale

Scale Item/variables

Sources from previous research

Item 19: Shared organizational values, beliefs, attitudes, and behaviours (i.e. firm culture).

Hall (1992)

Item 20: Organizational policies (e.g., recruitment, compensation, reward, and training) designed to acquire, develop, and retain the human talent of the firm.

Welbourne & Wright (1997)

Item 21: Organizational contract that firm has established with market-based participants (e.g., joint venture agreements, franchise agreement, distribution agreement)

Welbourne & Wright (1997)

Item 22: Organizational structure (i.e., the operating and reporting structure) of the firm.

Spanos and and Lioukas (2001)

Item 23: Brand name reputation corporate names or symbols used to distinguish one brand from another and to give a firm meaning and recognition in the market).

Hall (1992)

Item 24: Company's reputation (e.g., public perception on trustworthiness, social environment responsibility).

Hall (1992)

Item 25: Port services reputation (e.g., perception of the quality and reliability of the port services).

Hall (1992)

Table 1.7: Port Capabilities Scale

Scale Item/variables

Intangible Resources (Capabilities)

Sources from previous research

Item 26: The skills, creativity and know-how of employees based on primary activities (e.g. harbour operation system, berth operation system, handling operation system storage and yard operation system).

Ding (2009a)

Item 27: The skills, creativity and know-how of employees based on secondary activities (e.g. infrastructure and general administration affairs, HR management and IT).

Ding (2009a)

Item 28: The skills, and know-how of managers (e.g., intellectual and communication, planning and organizational skills).

Ding (2009a)

Item 29: The skills, creativity and know-how of manager based on primary activities (e.g., harbour operation, berth operation, handling operation, and storage and yard operation).

Ding (2009a)

Item 30: The skills, creativity and know-how of manager based on secondary activities (e.g. infrastructure and general administration affairs, HR management and IT).

Ding (2009a)

Item 31: Relationship that employees and manager have established and maintain with external constituents for the firm's benefit (e.g., customers, strategic alliances, supplier, etc.).

Spanos and Lioukas (2001); Fahy (2000); Welbourne and Right (1997)

Item 32: Routine (the series of repeatable or replicated operations, method, actions, tasks or functions).

Schroeder et al. (2002)

Table 1.8: Port Performance scale

Scale Item/variables

Sources from previous research

Item 33: Our port has been growing in total throughput volume.

Talley (2009)

Item 34: Our port has been growing in total number of TEU.

Talley (2009)

Item 35: Our port has been growing in total number of trade volumes.

Talley (2009)

Item 36: Our port profitability has been growing.

Spanos & Lioukas (2001)

CHAPTER TWO: PORT TANGIBLE AND INTANGIBLE RESOURCES

CHAPTER TWO: PORT TANGIBLE AND INTANGIBLE RESOURCES

1. **Introduction**

The focus of this study is to examine the relationship between the determinants of firm competitiveness and firm's performance in the port sector. In line with that, this chapter starts with a brief outline on some definitions and concepts relating to strategy and competitiveness. It is followed an explanation of the nature, origin and types of competitiveness. The next section discusses the determinants of firm and port competitiveness based on few related views, which include Industrial Organization (I/O) and New Industrial Organization, Revisionist, Austrian School of Economics, Profit Impact of Market Strategy and Resource-Based View. The discussion then continues with the explanation of firm and port competitiveness measurement and the past literature related to Malaysian port competitiveness. At the end of the chapter, a justification on the gap of the literature and the antecedents of firm and industry competitiveness are presented.

1. **Definitions of terms and concepts**

A few important terms and concepts needs to be highlighted in this study. They are namely: competitiveness, firm resources, firm performance.

2.2.1 Competitiveness

In general, competitiveness is defined as an ability of a firm, sub-sector or country to sell of supply of goods and services in a specific market. The word competitiveness is from the Latin word '*competere*', which means to strive together. In general, competitiveness is more relates to producing better and quality goods and services in a specific market compared to your competitors. In this regard, Geralli (2006) said "*What you have does not matter as much as what you do with what you have...*". This shows that sometimes a firm does not gain a competitive advantage not because they do not have the resources, but because they don't make use of these resources. This implies the important of identifying and utilizing the firm's resources in an effective and efficient manner.

Competitiveness also relates to an economic aspect. Economist relates firm competitiveness with the economic strength of a firm as compared to its competitors within the global market economy (Murths, 1998). Markets are distinguished relative to how many firms there are and whether the products of different firms are identical, and how easily it is for the firms to enter the actual market. Based from the economic point of view, competitiveness is about how firm differentiate themselves in term of products and services from the competitors and how the firm established entry barrier to avoid the entrance of other competitors to the market.

2.2.2 Firm Resources

Broad in scope, resources cover a spectrum of individual, social and organisational phenomena. A competitive advantage is generally based on the unique bundling of several resources (Sirmon, Hitt, & Ireland, 2007). Firm resources include all assets, capabilities, organizational processes, firm attributes, knowledge, information etc. controlled by a firm that enable a firm to conceive of and implement strategies that improve its efficiency and effectivenessDaft (1982). Firm resources can be divided into two dimensions of "tangible and intangible resources (Fahy, 2000). Tangible resources include those factors containing financial or physical value, which are reflected in the firm's financial statement. Intangible resources include all factors that are non-physical or non-financial sources. Below is the further explanation on firm tangible and intangible resources.

i. **Definition of Port Tangible Resources**

This section discusses the various definitions of firm and port resources, and empirical studies that examined a variety of resources effects on firm success, general theoretical and conceptual work in the extant literature that associated resources to competitive advantage and/ or firm performance.

According to Fahy (2000), firm resources are categorized into two types: tangible and intangible. Tangible resources include those factors containing financial or physical value, which are reflected in the firm's financial statement. Intangible resources include those factors that are nonphysical or nonfinancial, sources of economic benefit and are rarely, if at all, included in the firm financial statements.

Andersen and Suat Kheam (1998) argued that, generally, there is no disagreement over what encompasses tangible resources. Therefore, little effort is made to present an extensive amount of literature to define these resources. The resources definitions are drawn from Hofer and Schendel (1978) and Boulton, Libert, and Samek (2000). These definitions will be explained in detail below.

The tangible resources include: 1) Financial Assets which can be in a form of cash including currency (on hand or at the bank) earned from operations; raised financial capital-form of currency such as a financial loan or that resulting from a issuance of stocks or bonds (equity) and financial investments-investments such as money market funds, government-issued instruments, marketable securities, and company shares; and 2) Physical Assets which include building-tangible structure including factories, warehouses, stores, and showrooms including the location; equipment-any tool, piece of machinery, or other physical factor used to carry our particular business task or to produce, deliver, or install a product or service; and land-piece of real estate including the location thereof-held for productive use or investment.

In the context of port tangible resources, it can be categorised into three board categories. First category is port infrastructure and superstructure; second, is port physical aspect and third, technological applicability which includes information technology for capacity enhancement (UNCTAD, 2005).

(a) Infrastructure and Superstructure

The first port tangible resources are the port infrastructure and superstructure. These resources are considered to be one of the important resources for the port to run the operation. These resources are included: (1) basic port infrastructure, (2) operational port infrastructure, (3) port superstructure, and (4) port equipment. Basic infrastructure consists of maritime assess channel, port entrance, protective works including breakwaters and shore protection, sea locks, port inland transport such as road, tunnel , rail connection between hinterland and the port, and inland waterways within the port areas. Operational port infrastructure includes inner port channel, turning and port basins, quay wall, jetties and finger piers, aids to navigation, buoys and beacons. Port superstructure includes paving and surfacing, terminal lighting, parking areas, sheds, warehousing and stacking areas, tank farms and soils, offices, repairs shops and other building required for terminal operations. Port equipment include tugs, line handling vessels, dredging equipment, ship/shore handling equipment and cargo handling equipment (apron and terminal).

(b) Physical Aspect

In the physical aspect, two main features affect the site selection of ports. The first feature is the natural features, which include hydrographical data of region, availability of resources to build the port, tides and waves, weather and wind condition, hours of sunshine, rain level, natural harbour, and land availability. The second feature is the man-made features, which include accessibility to hinterland, availability of know-how, skilled labour for technical operation and construction of port (including dock labour), local legislation and environment of region and availability of port infrastructure.

(c) Technological Applicability

Port technology can be divided into two parts namely: (1) information technology and (2) intelligent transport system. As for the information technology in port, the first important thing is the Electronic Data Interchanges (EDI). According to Swatman and Swatman (1992), EDI is defined as a standard computer-to-computer exchange of inter-company business document and information. It allows cash flow, simplifies stock control, allow better customer services, reduce working capital, modernize business practice, and reduce communication costs.

As for the intelligent transport system (ITS), it gives a competitive advantage in terms of performance and efficiency. ITS system includes integrated information system, exit and entry control system, application of geographical information system (GIS) for yard planning, track and trace of container, and smart card at the entry and exit gate.

As for the purpose of resource construct and developing research hypothesis for this study, the definition of port tangible resources is based on the World Bank (2003), Hofer and Schendel (1978) and Boulton et al. (2000). Taking from these definitions, port resources for this study are included: 1) Physical Assets; 2) Financial Assets; and 3) Technological Assets.

ii. **Definition of Port Intangible Resources**

The definition of the intangible resources can be based on Lev (2001) who defined it as "a claim to future benefits that does not have physical or financial (a stock or bond) embodiment". In addition, Blair and Wallman (2001) defined it as "non-physical factors that contribute to or use in producing goods or providing service, or that are expected to generate future productive benefits for the individuals or firms that control the use of those resources". Hall (1992) has categorized intangible resources into two categories namely: 1) assets; and 2) skills.

For the purpose of this study, the classes of intangible resources are based on Hall (1992) and Barney (1991). They have divided the intangible resources into two major categories, namely 1) intangible resources that are non-physical asset and 2) intangible resources that are capabilities and skills. Intangible resources that are non-physical assets comprise of two major categories which are i) intellectual property assets; ii) organizational asset;

The intellectual property asset can be defined as an asset that is protected by law, or may be unpatented systems or invention held-in secret. They are largely derived from the intellectual property and consist of:

(a) Copyright

Copyright does not protect inventive ideas but rather legally protect embodiment or expression of ideas; literature, dramatic, musical and artistic works, sound recording, pictorial, graphic and sculptural, films and broadcasts, and computer software may be copyrighted by law (Hodkinson, 1987).

(b) Patents

Patents are exclusive, legally protected property rights, which are granted by the state or its inventor in respect of useful, new, and inventive products and process (Brooking, 1996).

(c) Registered design

These are the legal protection of the novelty or the features of shape, configuration, pattern, or ornamentation of a two dimensional (e.g. fabric or print) or three (e.g., beverage bottle) commercial article (Brooking, 1996; Hall, 1992).

(d) Proprietary (or held-in secret) technology

This encompasses all forms of proprietary or held-in secret information, manufacturing, or other technology including software) specifically designed and/or developed to fir a firm's particular business model (Hall, 1992; Williamson, 1985).

(e) Trademark

According to Hall (1992), trademark includes registered, legally protected product, service, and corporate brands. Trademark is a sign, including devices, aspects of packaging, names, phrases, sounds, letters, words, signatures, pictures, scents, symbols, or logo used to distinguish the goods or services of one party from another (Brooking, 1996; Hall, 1992).

For the purpose to construct the intellectual property assets for this study, it will be based on the definition from Hall (1992) and Brooking (1996). The intellectual property assets are include only legally protected patents, proprietary (or held- in secret) technology, and legally protected trademark. Another category of non-physical asset is organizational assets. Brooking (1996) and Boulton et al. (2000) suggested that without strong organizational assets, firms will undermine expanded market and revenue opportunities, constrain productivity, deliver poor quality products and services and have inferior talent. For the study, organizational assets are categorised into four main groups and the explanation are as below:

(f) Contracts

Contract is defined as an agreement between two or more parties that create a legal obligation between the parties which is enforceable by law (Hall,1992); contracts include agency agreement, franchise agreement, licensing agreement, property leases, and distribution agreements (Hall, 1992; Brooking, 1996).

(g) Culture

Culture embodies the complex pattern of beliefs, expectation, ideas, values, attitudes, and behaviours shared by the firm, set its decision-making patterns, and distinguishes it from other firms (Hofstede, 1997; Itami, 1987; Robbins, 1998).

(h) Human resources management (HRM) policies

HRM policies comprise a firm's employee-related practices including hiring, compensation, education, incentives, rewards, and training (Lado, 1994).

(i) Organizational structure

Organisational structure is defined as an operating and reporting structure of the firm (Barney, 1991; Boulton et al., 2000; Grant, 2002). The structure includes authority, role and task definitions, accountability, and liaison devices (Galbraith, 2000).

(j) Reputational assets

It is which define as a valuable, intangible asset that allows a firm to achieve lasting profitability (Roberts, 2002). For the purpose of this study, three categories of reputation are highlighted. The first category is the brand name reputation category. Brands include product, service, and corporate names or symbols that are used to distinguish one brand from another and to give a firm meaning and recognition in the market(s) it serves (Aaker, 1986; Kamakura, 1991). The second category is the company reputation. The company reputation is the overall embodiment of moral status (Fombrun, 1990). The company reputation includes public perception of factors such as trustworthiness, investor credibility, workplace diversity, managerial credibility, social and environmental responsibility, and regulatory accountability (Hall, 1992; Weigelt & Camerer, 1988). The third category is service reputation. It is the public perception of product/service innovations, product/service quality and reliability, and overall product/service image (Hall, 1993; Weigelt & Camerer, 1988). For the purpose of this study, the organisational assets construct will be based from Hall (1992), Welbourne and Wright (1997) and Spanos and Lioukas (2001).

The second type of intangible resources is port skills and capabilities. Based on all the resource constructs that constitute the RBV, capabilities remain the most difficult to define, having been operationalized in multiple and inconsistent ways (Hoopes, Madsen, & Walker, 2003). Day (1994) defined capabilities as a bundle of skills and accumulated knowledge. However, it is also referred as an organizational process (or routines) such as R&D activities, marketing, or customer service. Capabilities can be best understood as those factors that are built upon or are reflective of know-how, both tacit and explicit, which individuals and teams possess and exercise, including routines (Fahy, 2000).

However for the purpose of this study port capabilities are based on Ding (2009b) which categories capabilities into two major categories. First category is employee and managerial know-how, which based on primary activities and second is employee and managerial know-how, which based on secondary activities. However, another two more categories, which are included after the factor analysis test, are the relational skills ability of employees and managers and routine activities skills of the employees and managers. The item of the relational ability skills was taken from Fahy (2002), Spanos and Lioukas (2001), Welbourne and Wright (1997) whiles the item for routine activities skills of the employees and managers are taken from Schroeder, Bates, and Junttila (2002). Below is the explanation of the four types of the capabilities.

a) Primary activities and secondary activities.

For primary activities are include employee and manager activities which encompasses capabilities and skills in handling harbour operation system, berth operation system, handling operation system, storage and yard operation, traffic links to outskirts and customer services capabilities. While the secondary activities include employee and manager capabilities and skills based on the supports activities, which include capabilities in infrastructure and general administration affair, capabilities in human resource management and capabilities in IT management system.

b) Managerial know-how

Managerial know-how encompasses the intellectual, tactfulness, communicative, planning, and organizational skills of managers. Managerial know-how for primary and secondary activities is similar with the employee know-how, which is mentioned above. However, for managers, other skills are added and these are including intellectual, planning, communication and organisational skills.

c) Relational abilities

Relational abilities include relationships that employees and managers have established and maintained with external constituents (i.e., partners, customers, suppliers, government bodies) for the advantage of the focal firm (Charan, 1991; Hall, 1992).

d) Routines

Routines activities are the series of repeatable or replicated operations, method, actions, tasks or functions. The organizing principles of work facilitate identification of beginning and end states and imply all of the steps necessary to fulfil work activities in between (Nelson & Winter, 1982). Although routines may be codified (e.g. in manuals), they are largely become flows of tacit know-how embedded within the firm, which are exercised by individuals, across teams, and the firm at large, helping to facilitate what the firm does and how it does it (Nelson & Winter, 1982; Zollo & Winter, 1999).

2.2.3 Firm and Port Performance

In general, the purpose of this study is to apply the Resource-Based View in determining the relationship and the influence port's resources and capabilities on port performance. The following section discusses the measurement of firm and port performance. It will also highlight few different approaches of firm and port performance measurements that were suggested in the strategic management and transportation literature.

a. **Firm performance**

Though the terms competitive advantage and performance are often used interchangeably, Porter (1985) argued that the two constructs are acknowledged to be conceptually distinct. In general, competitiveness of a firm is measured based on its own performance, as argued by Rumelt and Teece (1994). Performance is conceptualized as the rents a firm accrues as a result of the implementation of its strategies. Thus, in measuring firm competitiveness, indicators relating to critical success factors for the firms' survival are used as a proxy.

According to Tovey (2001) firm performance indicators are various measures used by a firm to assess its performance on various activities that the firms indulge in. Performance indicators specify the type of evidence needed by the firm to demonstrate that strategic and operational plans are achieved as desired. Langen, Nijdam, and Horst (2007) specified that there are mainly three functions of performance indicators: 1) they provide management information for organization, 2) they serve to compare performance (of organizations and other units, such as countries) and, 3) they are used to communicate with relevant stakeholders.

Based on the literature, firm performance can be measured using various types of indicators. One of the most popular and widely accepted approach in strategy-performance studies (Geringer & Hebert, 1989). Some of the examples of the financial measurements are return on assets (ROA), return on investment (ROI), and return on sales (ROS). These indicators have been used in the previous studies (Bromiley, 1986; Jacobson, 1987; Palepu, 1985). Financial measures are important to determine the firm's performance this is done by comparing the performance level of various business units by using the standardized lines(Sieger, 1992). However, the financial measures only measure the tangible resources and these indicators often do not result in valid valuation of intangible resources (Huselid, 1995).

Other measures are using market-based measurement and it is also known as market value added (MVA). These measurements of firm's performance have received considerable attention in the literature (Amit & Livnat, 1988). According to Tully (1994), this is one of the most accurate measures of evaluating how well a firm increase the shareholder's wealth. Beside the quantitative measurements, firm's performance also could be accessed through the qualitative measures. These are include the subjective areas of performance such as ethical behaviour, stakeholder satisfaction with performance, customer satisfaction, and management satisfaction with performance (Parnell, Lester, & Menefee, 2000), employee satisfaction, delivery performance, process improvement, measures of material and parts delivery time, throughput time, due-date performance, quality and inventory levels (Hendricks & Singhal, 1996; Parnell et al., 2000).

In measuring performance, many firms usually employed multiple performance measures as appose to a single performance measure. By using multiple performance measures firms would be able to assess and evaluate firm competitiveness and performance in a more comprehensive manner. In the study on firm performance measurement of Malaysian firms, (Jusoh & Parnell, 2008) have used financial indicators such as sales growth and return on asset (ROA) and the result of their study found that Malaysian firms emphasized more on the use of financial measures of organizational performance as compared to other non-financial measurement.

b. **Port Performance**

As discussed earlier in the first chapter, with the globalization of trade, ports faced increased competition. Hence, it became more important to access the performance of one port in relation to its counterparts. However, due to the differences in the port's ownership, as well as different regulatory environment, a number of different approaches and performance indicators were suggested in the transportation literature.

Traditionally, port performance indicators (PPI) is measured based on the productivity of the port terminal since terminals are the most important function of ports. The classic monograph on port performance indicators is provided by UNCTAD (1976) which used indicators such as berth occupancy, revenue per ton of cargo, and capital equipment expenditure per ton of cargo. However, recently, port can be no longer act as a stand-alone entity, the functions of port and terminal have been expanded and turn into a cluster of economic activities.

Previous port literature are also has focused on measuring efficiency because the role of ports has been recognised as merely being nodes between land transport and sea transport and the virtue of ports are understood as being cost- and time-efficient operation (Talley, 2009). As highlighted by Brooks (2006), performance of ports has focused on measuring efficiency while other transport modes such as air, road and rail has put a greater emphasis on external perspective such as customer orientation, reliability and services. Since port have been developed into cluster activities where cargo handling, logistics, forwarding activities, stevedoring activities, bunkering and warehousing port related manufacturing, port performance should be measured based from these activities as the evaluation are more comprehensive (Pallis et al., 2008).

Langen et al. (2007) categorized port performance measurement into three major groups. The measurements of port performance are basically dependent on the nature of the firm's business or activities in a port. The first group is encompassed cargo transfer product firms. This group of firms includes terminal operating companies, towage, pilotage and bunkering firms. To this group of firms, the measurement of port performance is based on throughput volume and ship waiting time. The second group is the logistics services providers, transport firms and forwarders. In this group of firms, the port performance measurement is based on the value added in logistics. The third group is the port authority and utility providers for manufacturing. The port performance measurement is also based on value added and investment level in port-related manufacturing.

According to Langen et al. (2007), even though there are many indictors for measuring port performance, most widely used measurement for port performance is the throughput volume. However, the usage of throughput volume as a port performance indicator has few limitations. First, throughput volume does not tell much about the economic impact of a port. Second, growth of the throughput volume is mainly explained by the international trade flows, and not by the performance of a port. As ports deal with many types of cargoes such as bulk cargoes, liquid cargoes, general cargoes, break-bulk cargoes and containers, it is difficult to compare port performance rigorously by throughput (Slack, 2007).

For container port, the popular port performance indicator is based on total number of TEU. TEU or twenty –foot equivalent units is a standard unit for describing a ship's cargo carrying capacity and this is for the measurement of containerised cargo, which is equal to one standard 20 ft. (length) × 8 ft. (width) × 8.5 ft. (height) container (approximately 39 m3) (Talley, 2009). Meanwhile, Talley (2009) argued that port performance measurement can also be categorized based on the type of the port. For a single port perspective, port performance is measured not only based on the technical efficiency (whether a port is technically efficient) but also whether it is effective in providing throughput. Effectiveness is concerned with how well the port utilizes its available resources and provides throughput services to its users.

According to the same sources, the economic operating objectives of a port are classified as either efficiency or effectiveness objective. For example, the port efficiency operating objective includes the technically efficiency objective and this is done by maximizing throughput in the employment of a given level of resources (exhibited by port's economic production function). Another type of port efficiency is the cost efficiency objective and this was achieved through maximizing cost in the provision of a given level throughput (exhibited by the port's economic cost function).

In contrast, performance evaluation for the multiport perspective is much more different. This is because ports operate in different economic, social, and fiscal environment and because ports also have different economic objectives (Sukyens, 1986). Thus, for the evaluation of multiport performance, the technical efficiency of ports have generally been conducted by using frontier statistical models. These models are used to investigate the relative technical inefficiency of ports. Specifically, they relate the throughput (outputs) to the resources (or inputs) utilized by a group of ports to investigate which of these ports are technically efficient or inefficient relative to each other. The frontier statistical technique, data envelopment analysis (DEA) has often been used in the multiport technical performance evaluations.

One of the examples is Tongzon (2001), who used DEA to investigate the relative technical efficiency of sixteen international ports comparing two output variables with six input variables. The total output variables were the total number or TEUs loaded and unloaded (cargo throughput) and the number of TEUs moved per working hour (ship working rate). The input variables were (1) the number of crane, (2) the number of container berths (3) the number of tugs, (4) the ship delay time, (5) the terminal are, and (6) the number of port authority employee.

Based on the previous literature, there are many indicators used to evaluate port performance; however, the most widely used by leading ports are total throughput, port turnaround time, total number of TEUs, port profitability and other financial indicators (Langen et al., 2007). For this study, only three indicators of measuring port performance are used. These are total throughput, total number of TEUs and port's profitability. Port profitability is used for this study because the previous literature in the resources-based view has also empirically examined profitability measure as a function of firm competencies (Carolis, 2003; Hitt, Hoskisson, Ireland, & Harrison, 1991; Markides & Williamson, 1994). Port total throughput and TEUs are used in this study as these indicators are popularly used in the previous literature to measure port performance and competitiveness.

3. The Nature and the Origin of Competitiveness

The literature on competitiveness could be traced back to the 18th century in the earliest works of two scholars who discussed factors to become a successful and competitive nation. The first scholar was Adam Smith, a Scottish economist and popular with the book who wrote 'The Wealth of Nations' in 1776.Adam Smith stated that nations have absolute advantage when they have four input factors namely; land, capital, natural resources and labour. In order for a nation to become competitive, Smith emphasized,it is importance that it become lowest-cost producer (Krugman, & Obstfeld, 2003).

Later, another scholar, David Ricardo expanded Smith's idea of the nation's competitiveness by introducing ideas on comparative advantage and free trade among countries. Ricardo (1812) argued that a country that has resources, highly skilled labour will be more productive as compared to those countries that have less resources and unskilled labour. His work has been generally recognised as the origin of the general theory of international trade. Ricardo asserted that trade enabled a country to specialize and make full use of comparative advantage by varying production technologies between countries.

The argumentation of the concept of competitive nation was concluded by the introduction of a new concept known as the endowment theory. This theory is developed by Ohlin in 1933 and later extended by Huckster in 1949. They refined Ricardo's theory by incorporating the idea that countries can be an exporter of a product or service if they have abundant and cheap resources for production. Resources include land, skilled and unskilled labour and capital. Only by utilizing cheaper resources, a country would have advantages in the production of quality products or services over other countries.

The idea of comparative advantage was criticized by Leontif (1953)after an empirical research. Leontief came out with the idea that a country with the highest capital-per worker has a lower capital ratio and should be an export country. From these traditional trade theories, the idea of competitiveness has attracted attention of academic and non-academic scholars. These theories have provided valuable insights into the reasons for industry and trade successes among nations. However, the doctrine of competitiveness took a new dimension from 1960's onwards. Whilst earlier writers focused on the competitiveness of nations and industries, the concept has been more applied in the context of firms. At the firm level, most argument of competitiveness commonly focused on sources of firm's competitive advantage. They also provide several techniques and framework for analysing firms' competitiveness.

There are similarities between to the concept of competitiveness between the nation, industry and the firms. Based on the original concept of nations, the main idea was that was how to become competitive, production should be of the lowest cost possible with differentiating of products and services, and specialization. These three main elements were introduced by Michael Porter in the 1980's, formerly known as generic strategies which include low cost strategy, product differentiation and focus.

4. Source of Competitive Advantage

The debate on competitiveness was deepened at the firm level by the initiatives of several scholars. At the early stage, scholars differs in their views of the sources of firm competitive advantage. For example, Learned, Christiensen, Andrew, and Guth (1969) deepened the competitiveness debate when they emphasized on the context of organization in a firm. Competitiveness of a firm can be achieved if a firm assimilates all the elements; structure, system, culture, value, attitude to risk, key processes, people, technology and capital in its strategic planning. Thus, firms and industries must be able to integrate all these ingredients in its systematic strategy and structure as well as its holistic planning to become successful (Rumelt, 1974).

During the early 1960's and early 1970's, the development of analytical tools to assist management decisions became more accepted. Strategic tools and models were specifically designed to enable companies to analyse their competitive environment in which they operated. One of the important contributions is by the Harvard Business School and the Boston Consulting Group in 1973. A 'Portfolio Analysis model' was introduced a business tool to access firm's competitiveness. It was based on the concept that, the success of a company's business units can measured based on the company's market growth and market share relative to its largest competitor. Market growth serves as a proxy for industry attractiveness. However, the relative market share works as a proxy for firm competitive advantage. The growth-share matrix model shows the business unit position as compared to the other business unit within the firm.

Later, Andrew (1971) introduced SWOT analysis model that focused on a company's strengths, weaknesses, opportunities and threats. The acceptance of SWOT Analysis lies in its simplicity and its clear categorization of each of the elements of a company's internal and external operating environment. The debate on the sources of firm's competitive advantage became more aggressive in the 1980's with the involvement of Michael Porter of the Harvard Business School. His central idea of firm competitiveness originates from the theory of innovation. He generated the idea of firm competitiveness based on three major strategies, which are popularly known as 'generic strategy'. These strategies include low cost, product differentiation and focus. Firms can apply these strategies singularly or in combination to compete with the other participants in the industry and to sustain competitive advantage (Porter, 1980).

Another significant contribution by Porter is his argument on the attractiveness of firm's industry will directly affect the firm performance and competitiveness. This draws upon industrial organization (I/O) economics (Structure-Conduct-Performance) to derive five forces that determine the competitive intensity and therefore attractiveness of a market. The framework is known as Porter Five Forces. This framework explained that the performance of an industry depends on the level of opportunities and threats and will affect the potential performance of a firm (Porter, 1980). It has been applied to a diverse range of problems, which includes helping firms and businesses become more profitable and more competitive.

Several scholars have further explored the concept of firm competitiveness during the rise of multinational companies in the eighties. The idea also originated from the idea of innovation introduced by Schumpeter in 1934. Technological innovation is one of the driving forces or main sources of multinational firms to gain global competitive advantage. According to Levitt (1993), technology helps firms determine human preferences, and thus would enable multinational firms produce standardized products and apply economies of scales which will ensure higher profit and competitive advantage. Later, within the same view, Prahalad and Hamel (1990) emphasised on the importance of technology as a core competency for global firms to achieve competitive advantage. Some of the scholars that are share the same views on technological innovation are Stopford and Badenfuller (1994) and (Hamel & Prahalad, 1994).

Competitiveness of a global firm was expanded with the new perspective. Ohmae (1985) stipulated that firms competitiveness is about how firm conduct its business strategy and offers a better value to consumers in the most effective and sustainable way. Firm compete within the global competitive environment if they utilize the concept of 3 C's, which are commitment, creativity and competitiveness.

Competitive advantage could also be achieved by exploiting economies of scale through global volume advantage (Hout, Porter, & Rudden, 1982), whereby sustaining a winning position can be achieved through a large, timely investment, and managing interdependently to achieve synergies across different activities in a firm. In contrast, Rumelt (1984) argued that in order to sustain competitiveness, the existence of barriers to imitation is required. This can be accomplished through an analysis of price factors, exchange rate, wages, and by the use of various non-price factors such as technology, design, quality and productive efficiency.

The wider scope of competitiveness of firms and industries has been clearly explained by the introduction of Porter's Diamond framework. This framework linked the gap between traditional theory, which emphasize the nation, and business management theories, which emphasize on firms. The framework provides a better understanding for determining the international success of a nation, industry and firm. Based from this framework,

Porter (1990) argued that an industry is competitive if the nation has provide the most positive environment for the firm within the industries to innovate. It also shows how important the industry and its environment are to the firm strategic planning and competitive position.

Instead of the influence of industry and environment, the concept of firm's cluster has also has been recognized as giving an impact towards the success of firms and industries. Using the same model of Diamond Framework, Porter (1998, 2000) argued that cluster affects competition by increasing the productivity capacity for innovation and productivity growth of a firm or industry. Within the clusters, all business firms, suppliers and associated institutions in a particular field are interconnected and this would encourage the formation of new business, support the innovation and could increase the productivity and performance of a firm.

In the 21st century, technological revolution and increasing globalization present major challenges to firms' ability to maintain their competitiveness. According to Hitts, Keats, and DeMarie (1998), success in the 21st century organization will depend first on building strategic flexibility. The development of strategic flexibility and competitive advantage requires exercising strategic leadership, building dynamic core competences, focusing and developing human capital, effectively using new manufacturing and information technologies, employing valuable strategies (exploiting global markets and cooperative strategies) and implementing new organization structures and culture (horizontal organization, learning and innovative culture, managing firm as bundles of assets).

According to Mathews (2006), with globalization the emergence of MNE's has brought a new perspective on firm's competitive advantage. The OLI theory (Ownership, Locational and Internationalization) explained how and why MNE's achieved competitiveness by accessing the resources through the internationalization strategy. It is a framework that sees MNEs as deriving advantages from their superior resources that they exploit abroad. Other sources of competitive advantage are the technology intensity, low labour cost, extra-national economies of scale, multinational customers and universality of customer needs (Hamel & Prahalad, 2012).

Based on the discussion on the sources of firm competitive advantage, it is clear that the major source of competitive advantage is dependent on firm's innovation because through innovation firms will be able to select the best strategies for the firm. Thus, differentiation is one of the strategy that encouraged firms to be innovative. Firm's innovation such as technological innovation is an important source of competitive advantage especially for multinational firms. Using technological innovation, firms would be able to achieve higher profit by producing global product through applying economies of scale. Besides, firms can achieve competitive advantage by looking into the attractiveness of its industry structure and its external environment. Furthermore, the concept of industry cluster or 'hub', which emphasized the interconnectedness between business, suppliers and other associated institutions, may be a source of competitive advantage.

5. **Types of Competitiveness**

After the brief explanation on few concepts of strategy and competitiveness, this chapter attempts to explain the types of competitiveness based on the previous literature.

2.5.1 Nation Competitiveness

In general, nation competitiveness is related to national prosperity and it can be determined by the number of resources such as the nation's natural environment such as labor pool, interest and currency rates. The nation competitiveness is also dependent on the capacity of its industry to innovate and upgrade, its strong domestic rivals, number of home-based suppliers and local demands. In the next section, some definitions of nation competitiveness is discussed.

a. **Definition and concept of nation competitiveness**

Based on the previous discussion, the oldest school of thought views competitiveness of a nation is the ability of that nation to become the lowest cost producer by taking advantage of its abundant resources. From this central idea, a comprehensive definition of competitiveness of nation was proposed by several important institutions which is related to nation competitiveness. For example, a general definition of competitiveness can be attributed to the International Institute for Management Development's World Competitiveness Yearbook which defined national competitiveness as a set of institutions, policies, and factors that determine the level of productivity of a country (Garelli, 2009). Level of productivity of a nation, in turn, will determine the sustainability and prosperity of a nation.

Another definition can be attributed to the US Competitive Council (1992) which has defined nation competitiveness as *"a capacity to produce goods and services that correspond to the demand of the international market while giving to the citizens living standards that grow and can be preserved in the long time"*.

This definition implies that the vital goal of a nation is to improve the living standard of its citizens. This is similar to the concept due to Scott and Lodge (1985) who referred to national competitiveness as an ability of a country to create, produce, distribute the product or services in the international trade while utilizing its resources to get higher returns. Most of the new perspectives on nation competitiveness are based on Porter's works in the early eighties and nineties. He emphasized the concept of nation comparative advantage, which means that nation, or industry only can succeed when they produce at the lower cost relative to others.

Considerable work has shown that competitiveness of a nation is usually measured based on the national level of productivity (Porter, 1990, 2008). The measurement of productivity relies on the quality and the technical efficiency of a product. Porter (1990) commented that the determination of a nation's standard of living depends on the ability of its domestic firms to achieve high level of productivity. However, sustainable productivity growth requires a nation to continuously raise product quality and improve product technology. In order to achieve nation competitive advantage, support from the government is required in term of promoting a competitive and conducive environment to improve quality, innovation and productivity.

In contrast, Krugman (1994) argued that competitiveness is not related to productivity and international competition. Government can promote nation competitiveness by exercising new strategy such as by practicing protectionism or currency devaluation, discriminatory customs and dues, administrative pressures, direct legislative control, exchange control and bilateral trade treaties.

Based on the definitions detailed above, generally, there are three perspectives of national competitiveness. First, national competitiveness is about the level of productivity of a nation and the level of productivity will determine the rate of return obtained by investments in an economy. From the high level of investment, a nation will be able to achieve high growth and competitive advantage. Secondly, competitiveness is also defined as an ability of a nation to increase its national income by producing competitive goods and services in response to the market. By doing this, a nation will improve its quality and standard of living of its citizens. The first and second definitions share a common spirit, that is, the creation of a conducive environment to improve the prosperity of a nation. Thirdly, competitiveness of a nation is not about productivity, but rather on national strategies to compete involving government policies on macro and micro economic and protectionism policy.

b. Measurement of Nation Competitiveness

After defining nation competitiveness in the previous section, the next section below is about to explain the measurement of nation competitiveness. There is no single method of measuring nation competitiveness and the determinants of nation competitiveness are complex and many. According to Porter et al., (2002), nation competitiveness can be measured based on four broad categories. The first measurement is based on the general performance of a nation. The general performance of a nation can be measured by gross national product (GNP) per capita, average annual growth of GNP per capita and standard deviation of income distribution. The second measurement is based on the level of macroeconomic and market dynamics. It includes investment and growth in productivity, general trade dimensions, export competitiveness and structure, tariff policy, and government involvement in economy. The third measurement is based financial measures and some of the examples are growth of foreign debt, present net value of foreign debt and average annual rate of GDP deflator and so on. The fourth category is based on the level of investment for nation's infrastructure such as information and communications network, physical infrastructure and socio-political stability.

Besides competitiveness measurement, another important aspect, which is related to nation competitiveness, is about the model of nation competitiveness. One of the most comprehensive models on nation competitiveness was developed by Porter (1990) and it was called the "Diamond model". Based on this model, the major determinants of nation competitiveness encompassed four country specific determinants namely: factors conditions, demands condition, related and supporting industries, and firm strategy, structure, and rivalry. Two exogenous parameters namely: government and chances are very important factors in such a model. This model has been widely used in analysing nation and industry competitiveness (Bellak & Weiss, 1993; Hodgetts, 1993).

However, this model has been criticized because it failed to integrate the effect of multinational firms' activities (Chang Moon, Rugman, & Verbeke, 1995, 1998).Also this model cannot be applied to measure competitiveness of a developing countries (Bellak & Weiss, 1993). Due to these views, Porter's Diamond model has been extended to a new model named "Generalized Diamond" model whereby the multinational activities are formally incorporated. According to Cho and Moon (1998) nation competitiveness is a nation's competitive position in the international market among nations of similar economic development.

Based on the discussion above, there are several variables to measure nation competitiveness. These variables include nation productivity, government roles, innovation and skills, real exchange rate, productivity growth, competitive performance, potential and process, GNP per capita, macroeconomic and financial competitiveness, investment infrastructure, and intellectual capital. Most of the measures are based on quantitative indicators.

2.5.2 Industry Competitiveness

The second level of competitiveness is at the industry level and this concept is quite similar to the earlier one. According to Martin, Westgren, and van Duren (1991), industry competitiveness is about possessing and sustaining profitability as well as gaining and maintaining market share in the domestic or foreign market.

There are several previous studies, which have tried to compare the relative competitiveness of countries for a specific industry by using specific measurement to test the competitiveness of the industry. For example Peterson and Barras (1987) measured competitive index for tradable products and services across industries and countries. They calculated an index of competitiveness based on publicly traded airlines and aerospace enterprises. The index used, among others, financial ratios, asset utilization, and productivity, financial stability, earning protection, liquidity and market valuation. Yamin, Mavondo, Gunasekaran, and Sarros (1997) did a survey of industry managers using the measurement of hypotheses and factors affecting competitive strategy, organizational innovation and performance.

Other studies on nation's competitiveness are from Sakakibara and Porter (2001) who used a broad sample from the Japanese industry to explore the impact of industry competitiveness on performance of international trade. In this study, they found that home market has an impact to overall international competitiveness of a nation. Thus, it shows that competitiveness within the industry do affect the competitiveness of a nation.

The contribution of Michael Porter through his books "*Competitive Strategy*" (Porter, 1980) and "*The Competitive Advantage of Nations*" (Porter, 1990) need to be highlighted to explain the concept of competitive advantages of industry. One of the reasons why one should highlight these two books is that both works has used the 'industry' as a unit of analysis. Furthermore, the success of individual firms was largely dependent upon their ability to operate within the structure of the industry. Porter (1980) argued that an industry's competitiveness is dependent upon five major forces or factors. These are 1) the threat of new entrants, 2) the threat of substitute products or services, 3) the bargaining power of suppliers, 4) the bargaining power of buyers and 5)rivalry among existing competitors. Porter (1980) also argued that a company's strategy is responsible for the creation of competitive advantage, but the strategy must be assessed within the structure of the industry in which it operates. Therefore, the 'rules' and influencing factor of industry becomes the fundamental for the strategic actions of a company.

Porter (1990a) noted that all the factors in the Diamond model act as a system that creates the climate in which a nation's firm compete. However, the competitive advantage within an industry cannot be developed without the availability of resources and skills. Central to Porter's Diamond thesis was the provision of a framework that facilitated an explanation of how the presence of specific conditions inherent in a nation makes certain industries successful. As noted, the ability of a nation to create higher standards of living depends ultimately upon the competitiveness of its industries and companies. Porter (1990a) maintained that understanding the determinant of productivity growth is based on understanding how companies and industries improve their competitiveness.

Porter (1990) also stated the role of government in influencing the effective working of the determinants of industry and nation competitiveness. He added that the manipulation of national attributes can also create an industry environment, which is conducive to high level of productivity through its internal working. Based on the same sources, he also argued that the government can strengthen and reinforce the conditions within their control. For example, the government can control taxation and regulatory conditions to achieve nation and industry competitiveness.

According to Porter (2008), the systematic nature of Diamond promotes the concept of clustering a nation's competitive industry. In Porter's idea, the successful cluster in an industry are linked through vertical and horizontal integration of relationships which facilitate buyer/supplier and common customers and technological relationships, magnify and accelerate the process of factor creation. Porter (1990) argued that the formulation of clusters fosters mutually supporting benefits for industries that flow backward, forward or horizontally.

The competitiveness of a cluster can be assessed by comparing the level of performance of the same industry with another country or region, which there is an open trade. The performance of a cluster can be measured based on the level of productivity of firms in the industry, level of capacity for innovation and the numbers of new business formation that supports innovations and expands the cluster (Porter, 2008).

Competitiveness in an industry can also be derived from the value chain concept. Value chain promotes the industry's competitiveness by giving the value added to the customers through firm's discrete activities (Porter, 1980). Porter noted that a company's value chain for competing in an industry is embedded in a larger stream of activities in what he termed as a 'value system'. The value chain also provides a tool for understanding the sources of inefficiency and the cost advantage in an industry.

2.5.3 Firm Competitiveness

The ideas of firm competitiveness originated from the "*Theory of the Firm*" and was based on Micro Economics perspective which emphasized on costs and prices of a product or service. By fixing the right cost and price, firm will be able to determine and maximize its profit through economies of scale. Cost is a good indicator of firm competitiveness and this theory gained wide acceptance. However, the theory of firm and cost competitiveness have its limitations. The rise of strategic management and marketing scholars has brought a new perspective on firm competitiveness. Unlike the economic discipline, recent researches in the management field suggest that non-price factors are equally important determinants of competitiveness. Another name for non-price factors is the intangible resource factors and these include human resource, skills and capabilities, technical, managerial and organisational, relationships with other bodies, customers, suppliers, public private research institutes, and other firms (Clark & Guy, 1998).

While there are many views and arguments that may contribute to the idea of firm competitiveness, the most influential argument would probably be from strategic management. One of the best views is that Porter who emphasized on the importance to incorporating both firm's internal and external factors need which allow firms to compete successfully. The internal factors are (i) factors condition which include the availability of skilled employees, firm infrastructure; (ii) the demand condition factors which include the number of demand of a products or services of the industry; (iii) numbers of supporting industries which include numbers of suppliers, vendors and distributors; and (iv) firm strategy, structure, and rivalry. Together, these four factors create the context in which firms are born and compete.

The concept of firm competitiveness also can be viewed from the customer perspective. In which a competitive firm is one that can identify and fulfil the needs of targeted customers more efficiently and effectively than its rivals (Buckley, Pass, & Prescott, 1988). Likewise, Porter (1990) suggested that, to gain a competitive advantage in the market place, firms must be able to offer the lowest cost than its competitors and also able to differentiate their products or services. By offering the lowest cost, a firm will be able to create greater customer value as compared to its competitors. Product differentiation can be in the form of adding product quality standards, adding desirables structures or characteristics, specialization, improving production process through technology and innovation and improving capabilities to compete in more sophisticated industries (Ambastha & Momaya, 2004).

The ideas of firm competitiveness have been expanded to new dimension by another group of scholars which known as Resource-Based View. This group emphasized the importance of firm's resources and capabilities. However they have shown that firms would be able to sustain their competitive advantage when they have organizational resources and skills that are valuable, rare, inimitable, and non-substitutable. This group emphasized the importance of firms' intangible resources which can be in the form of firms' competencies and capabilities.

2.5.4 Port competitiveness

Based on the detailed explanation of the types of competitiveness, this sub-chapter attempts to explain the concept and definition of port competitiveness. Even though port competitiveness seems to have different meaning, the theoretical grounding would be based on the earlier concept of competitiveness discussed in the previous section.

In general, a port (or seaport) is a place at which the transfer of cargo and passenger to and from waterways and shore occurs. A port may be a cargo port (handling only the transfer cargo), a passenger port (handling only the transfer of passengers), or a combination of both (handling the transfer of both cargo and passengers). Similarly, Talley (2009) described a port as an economic unit which it provides a transfer service as opposed to producing a product as for a manufacturing firm.

However, a port has recently become more than a centre of transferring goods and cargoes. In the early eighties, a significant role of port has been extended to the multimodal and logistics centre to facilitate international trade activities. The role of a multifunctional port has been highlighted by Notteboom (2004)in which he defined a port as an area or place that has been developed into logistics and industrial centre, transhipment and industrial hub which can be accessed through maritime and hinterland.

Looking at the crucial important of port to the nation's economic and growth, scholars have tried to understand the factors that contributed to port competitiveness. Most agreed that productivity is not the only indicator in evaluating port competitiveness. They argued that port competitiveness includes various economic and non-economic indicators. A broad definition of port competitiveness is derived from Frankel (1987)who stressed that ports can be competitive if they can differentiate their products or services offered by using differentiation and focus strategy and this may attract more clients.

In other view, Talley (2009) defined port competitiveness as a port's competitive position. He further explained that port competitiveness could be evaluated in terms of growth, market share, and diversification of its traffic volume. For discussing further explanation on port competiveness, the term port competition need to be defined first. According to Talley (2009), port competition is categorized into inter-or intra port competition. He described inter-port competition as a competition between different ports and intra-port competition as competition among terminals within the same ports. A broad concept of port competition can also be derived from Haezendonck and Notteboom (2002) who defines port competition as a competition between port terminal operators who are involved in the transport chain and that the competition is based not only on tangible asset but also on provision of service. In this study, port competitiveness is referred to as inter-port competition where the purpose is to evaluate the relationship between port resources and port competitiveness among several major terminal ports operators in Malaysia.

From the 1990's up until the late 2000's, port researchers are still differing on what the major factors of port competitiveness are. The recent trends within the port industry which include the rise of the containerization, emergence of global liners, increasing size of vessels and the recent development of port technology and port IT system have changed the perspective of port competitiveness. However among the factors that have been identified to be the major contribution to competitiveness are geographical and locational factors (Starr, 1994; UNCTAD, 1992), technology (Hoyle, 1999; Murphy, Dalenberg, & Daley, 1991), port in information system (UNCTAD, 1992; Gordon et al, 2005), technical infrastructure of the port such as handling equipment and ICT (Gordon et. al, 2005), international politics, social and economic environment (Bookbinder & Tan, 2003; UNCTAD, 1992), and port policy (Al-Bisher, Gray, & Stead, 2012; Enzo, 2013). However, there is also other factors which include port efficiency (Bang, Kang, Martin, & Woo, 2012; Cullinane, Ping, & Teng-Fei, 2005; Pagano, Wang, Sanchez, & Ungo, 2013; Schøyen & Odeck, 2013; Tongzon & Heng, 2005; Wang, Knox, & Lee, 2013).

Even though previous research on port competitiveness emphasized more on issues related to the port tangible resources, a number of research tended to focus on the aspect of intangible resources which encompassed port capabilities and competencies. These include cultural differences (Luo et al., 2001), port reputation (Wiegmans et al., 2008), port management (Lirn et al., 2004), service level (Peteraf, 1993), image marketing (Rozenblat, 2004), port ownership structure (Notteboom et al., 2012), availability of skilled employees, quality of logistic services (Feng et al., 2012), quality management practice (Cheng & Choy, 2013) port cooperative relationship (Low & Tang, 2012)as well as horizontal and vertical integration and concentric diversification (Parola et al., 2013).

There are many other views with regard to the elements and determinants of port competitiveness. In order to provide an overall perspective on firm and port competitiveness, the next section will explore the various theoretical views on firm and port competitiveness based on the six major schools of thought. These include the theoretical views based on Industrial Organisation (I/O) and New Industrial Organization, Revisionist, Austrian School of Economics, Profit Impact of Market Strategy and Resource-Based View.

2.6 Relationship of firm resources and performance

Scholars and practitioners have been trying to answer the question "Why are some firms better than others?". This is one of the most popular questions to which many scholars have different views or answers. The next section is to explain the previous literature on the determinant of firms and port competitiveness based on six major schools of thought. These are based on the Industrial Organisation (I/O), and New Industrial Organization, Revisionist, Austrian School of Economics, Profit Impact of Market Strategy, and Resource-Based View.

2.6.1 Relationship of firm resources and performance based on Industrial Organization (I/O) Perspective

The literature on firm competitiveness has been influenced and grounded by industrial organization economics. Industrial organization economics focuses on industry structure as the determinant of performance across industries. They stipulated that the success of a firm is determined by the industry structure itself. The structure of the industry depends on the few important condition such as demand for a product or services or the degree of technology (2004).

Mason (1939) was among the first scholars who found that there is a relationship between industry structure and firm performance. Based on the IO views, the industry structure that has an existence of barriers to entry will have impact on the performance of a firm (Bain, 1956). Barrier to entry is defines as anything that allows the existing firms to earn the higher profit without the competition of new firms. More importantly, barrier to entry involves a set of economic forces that create a difficulty to new competitors trying to enter the market. Examples of economics forces include government regulation such as intellectual property rights, or patent, subsidies for local firms, flag discrimination. All these forces require high financial costs to enter the market.

Another form of barrier to entry is the pricing strategy. This is one of the most popular strategies used by the larger firms to gain competitive advantage. The strategy is to lower the prices to a level that would prevent new entrants. This strategy is effective when a firm has cost advantage over potential new firms. A firm gains cost advantage through economies of scales and control over its production, thus at the same time drive up market prices (Bain, 1956).

Barrier to entry will create the element of monopoly within an industry. By having the elements of entry barriers firms should be able to increase their monopoly power and prevent other firms from gaining monopoly control and this will ensure that they continue to maintain their market dominance and increase market share. Industrial organisation emphasized the important roles of market power in competition and for positioning to be dominant player in the market.

The second characteristic an industry structure that influences the firm competitiveness are the number, the size, and the distribution of buyers and sellers. It is important to be a large firm relative to the market in order to attain productive efficiency and earn higher profit without the threat from new firms(Bain, 1968). Large firms will be able to take advantage of economies of scale by producing large quantities. The argument for the importance of large size to the firm was supported by Conner (1991) who found that firms need to be big because they can control substantial proportion of industry output and therefore, it can gain a greater monopoly power and be more competitive.

The third characteristic of the industry structure that yields competitiveness is the degree of product differentiation in the industry. Bain (1956) describes how firms try to produce products that are relatively unique that can differentiate them from others. Product differentiation can be in terms of product quality. Firms usually induce the perception of product quality by using advertisements. Advertisement is one of the mechanisms to induce customer loyalty for a certain brand. Firms can also differentiate themselves from their competitors by changing the characteristics of products or services. However, any change in the characteristics of the product supplied by one firm, whether real or imagined, may affect the shares of the total market demand that each firm is able to command (Lipczynski, Wilson, & Goddard, 2005).

These three major definitions have led to a broad and inclusive definition of entry barrier, which is incorporated in a quotation by Carlton and Perloff (1994). The quotation is provided below.

"Anything that prevents an entrepreneur from instantaneously creating a new form in a market, while a long run barrier to entry is a cost that must be incurred by a new entrant that incumbent do not (or have not had to) bear".

Besides the three elements in the market structure discussed previously, the industrial organization scholars introduced two other elements that influence the firm performance and competitiveness. The concepts of vertical integration and diversification of firms are among the elements of performance and competitiveness discussed in the literature. Vertical integration refers to the extent to which a firm is involved in different stages of the same production process whereas diversified firms produce a variety of goods or services for several distinct markets (Lipczynski et al., 2005). Vertically integrated firms have a greater certainty in obtaining supplies of raw materials or guaranteeing distribution outlets. They have opportunities to engage in certain types of anticompetitive practice (vertical restraints), which may be damaging to non-integrated rivals. Diversified firms may benefit from economies of scope and are less exposed to risk than their non-diversified counterparts because losses realized in one market can be offset against profits earned elsewhere (Lipczynski et al., 2005).

In explaining the importance of industry structure as a key determinant of the performance variance among firms competing in different industries, Bain (1956) introduced an important paradigm called structure-conduct-performance (SCP). The SCP paradigm explained the whole attributes within the industry structure which firm can follow to outperform rivals and achieve higher performance. In the SCP paradigm, industry's structure has certain attributes including industry concentration and barriers to entry, the number and relative size of firms, the existence and degree of product differentiation in the industry, and the overall elasticity of demand for the industry.

SCP paradigm explains how firms within the industry structure (S) conduct (C) or plan their strategies to achieve higher performance (P).Conduct can be seen in how firms determine their price or how much they spend on advertising which in turn determines the firm performance and profitability (Scherer, 1980). The SCP paradigm has been expanded by Hunt (1972) who introduced the concept of strategic group of firms within an industry. Strategic group is an approach to study factor affecting for different profitability within an industry. To date, strategic group is usually defined as a group of firms in the same industry following the same or similar strategies (Porter, 1980). The benefit of having the strategic group is to protect firms in a strategic group from entry of s of another group through means such as scale of economies, product differentiation, or distribution network (Caves & Porter, 1977). The basis for strategic group formation include firm size and industry concentration ratio, in manufacturing (such as capital intensity of plants), marketing (such as number of brands) and financing (such as leverage) (Hoskisson, Hitt, Wan, & Yiu, 1999).

However, despite the large number of studies on strategic group, this stream of research faces several criticisms. Barney and Hoskisson (1990) challenged two untested assertions in strategic group theory: (1) whether strategic group exist; (2) whether a firm's performance depends on strategic group membership. Besides, other researchers notablyWiggins and Ruefli (1995) found that stability of performance group membership is lacking. They questioned the efficacy of mobility barrier and thus, the predictive validity of strategic group.

a. **Relationship of port resources and performance - The Application of I/O Theory**

There have been extensive applications of the I/O theory in business and strategic management research. However, in port economic literature, a number of studies tried to apply some of the concepts in I/O. The port industry is characterized by relatively large government involvements. Ports are surrounded by substantial economic, regulatory and geographical entry barriers. In conceptualizing port entry barriers, Langen and Pallis (2007) identified three different categories of seaport entry barriers. The first seaport entry barrier can be in the form of an economic entry barrier which could cause higher switching cost and higher cost of investment to acquire capital and knowledge for the new entrants. These difficulties may cause the new entrants to suffer losses and makes entry unprofitable. The second category is institutional entry barriers, which can be in a form of restricted entrance for historical, ideological, commercial reasons and conditions of exclusive concessions. Finally, the third entry barrier is locational entry barriers, which include the unavailability of the land for entrants.

All the three types of entry barriers are very significant in the seaport industry. The existence of entry barrier in the seaport and maritime industry makes this industry difficult to access. In order to be able to access the market, firms have to follow regulations and procedures from the port authority. Instead, new firms must bear high financial cost to remain in the industry. Because of these characteristics, entry is difficult. This may be one of the reasons why existing firms or terminal operators in this industry are able to gain higher profit and why there is a severe shortage of terminal capacity (Olivier, 2005).

A typical example of institutional entry barriers is the concession agreement. Pallis et al. (2008) explained that the concession agreement started when there was a need for port authority to invest in terminals to accommodate transport flows. As described by Olivier, Parola, Slack, and Wang (2007), concessions is a trend which resulted from the advancement of containerisation and the development of container terminals.

In contrast Pallis et al. (2008) argued that concessions agreement can be part of a barrier to entry and at the same time can be a dominant entry mode for private firms to enter the seaport market. Example of major entry mode for private firms in the seaport market is through acquiring a concession agreement to provide terminal services. They also found that tender in the concession agreement may also lower entry barriers by ensuring transparency, absence of discrimination and exclusivity, and concessions for certain periods.

Requirement in concession procedures can create entry barriers and lower contestability of the market. For example, in order to win a concession, the private firm is required to have good track records, proven business experiences, technical and financial solvency and must have specific firm capabilities or core competencies (2008). Access to port markets thus remains limited to a number of terminal operating companies, which have developed competencies that are very difficult for non-incumbent firms to imitate. The characteristic of port market structure that only have few firms or terminal operators running the port businesses indicates the existence of monopoly power in the port industry.

In contrast to this view, Magala (2004) argued that the prevalence of port competitive environment and monopoly power in port industry is limited due to government intervention and market realities. In such environment, ports would not be able to increase their market share and gain sustainable profit by price fixing strategy but by enhancing its port innovation of port products and services as well as by delivering value-added services to customers within the supply chain in which they are embedded.

The discussion on the application of Industrial Organisation has been prolonged by few other scholars particularly in explaining the concept of market power and integration in the seaport industry. Market players in the seaport industry are selected based on their relationship among the maritime logistic chain and not because of their stand-alone competitiveness. In general, maritime logistic chain encompasses port authority as a government body, shipping companies as its principal customer and port terminal operator as the main supplier of throughput services.

Van de Voorde and Vanelslander (2009), observed a trend that shows that market players in the maritime logistic chain are trying to gain greater control over the chain through horizontal and vertical integration. Thus, it gives an implication to the broader concept of competitiveness strength of seaport, which is dependent on the various variables within the maritime logistic chain and not only on one particular firm or player.

Studies conducted by port scholars evaluated the effectiveness of vertical and horizontal integration among a few major players in the seaport industry. A successful example involved the China Ocean Shipping Group Companies (COSCO), which was originally a state-owned enterprise. COSCO has been transformed into a cooperation that was characterized by an impressive new range of horizontal and vertical linkages and has become one of the major container carriers in the world (Pinder & Slack, 2004). Another successful and most recent was the takeover of P&O Ports by Dubai Port Authority which was renamed as Dubai Port (DP) World (Van de Voorde & Vanelslander, 2009). Other successful companies include Hutchison Port Holdings (HPH), which obtained a market share of 15% of the worldwide throughput of more than 66 million TEU, on the total throughput of 485 million TEU.

The question, which was raised, was whether horizontal cooperation and vertical cooperation among players in the maritime industry results in more benefits and achieve the objective of the integration. In general, one of the reasons for integration is to achieve the economies of scale and scope. There are several examples of non-successful mergers operation among the major players. One of example of merger is between Nedlloyd and P & O in 1996. The major objective of the merger is to achieve economies of scale and to lower cost. However, the merger and the operation was not successful and the stated objective was not achieved (Van de Voorde & Vanelslander, 2009).

In conclusion, the competitiveness of firms in the seaport industry can be conceptually explained using ideas proposed by the Industrial Organisation. The position of seaport players which are embedded in the maritime logistic chain have encouraged them to apply the strategies proposed by the I/O. The application of the concept of entry barriers through concession agreement, market power and strategic group through the vertical and horizontal integration have been widely applied by the players in seaport industry in order to achieve and sustain competitive advantage.

2.6.2 Relationship of firm resources and performance based on New Industrial Organisation Perspective

Based on the previous discussion, the traditional I/O model emphasized firm competitive advantage based on external sources. However, this model has been expanded by the new group of scholars known as The New Industrial Organization. This group of scholars identifies that firms have a certain influence on the relationship between industry structure and a firm's performance (Hansen & Wernerfelt, 1989). The expanded model was introduced by Porter in 1980 and is known as the Five Forces Framework. This model has provides a useful analysis tool to assess the competitiveness and the attractiveness of an industry.

Like I/O economists, Porter (1980) paid a lot of attention to the industry structure. In this model, the degree of the competition within an industry can be determined using five structural parameters and this include: the current condition of the competition within the industry; the bargaining power of suppliers, bargaining power of buyers, threat of new entrants, and threat of substitute products or services.

The first structural force is the threat of new entrants, which focuses on the strength of an industry's barrier to entry. That is, it focuses on the favourability of industry barriers that may restrict the arrival of new entrants, thus protecting the industry's profit potential. Barriers to entry include economies of scale, product differentiation, customer loyalty to an established brand (Mintzberg, Ahlstrand, & Lampel, 1998). The higher the barrier to entry, the more likely firms within the industry will seek to tacitly collude to maintain those barriers, thus making it difficult for outsiders to gain entry, which preserves industry performance (Grant, 2002).

The second structural force is the threat of substitute products or services, focuses on the level of competition within and between industries. In industries where product or service substitute are available, industry profitability is protected. In industries where many product or service substitutes are readily available, industry profitability can suffer. Thus, competition depends on the extent to which products or services in one industry can be replaced by products or services from another (Digman, 1999).

The third structural force is the bargaining power of suppliers. It focuses on the relative power and control that supplier can or cannot require within an industry. If the suppliers are plentiful and commoditized, the choice and the bargaining power over price favour firms in the industry, which, in turn, positively impacts the overall industry performance.(Bernet, 1996).

The fourth structural force is the bargaining power of buyers, which focuses on the firm's customers and their relative purchasing power. Buyers attempt to bargain for lower prices while demanding higher quality from the producers of goods and services. Firms making concessions to buyers with bargaining power necessarily increase industry rivalry, which ultimately erodes industry profit margin (Digman, 1999).

The fifth force, which is the rivalry among existing competitors, which focuses on the competition of firms within an industry. Essentially, the fifth force seeks to explain the conduct of firms engaged in the battle for market share and performance. If there is intense rivalry in an industry, it will encourage firms to engage in price wars (such as competitive price reduction), investment in innovation and new products and intensive promotion (such as sale promotion and higher spending on advertising).

The important point from Porter's five forces is that they are a function of the industry. Furthermore, because the conduct of a firm is constrained by external structural forces, the favourability or unaffordability of the potential of a firm is influence by the attractiveness of the industry structure within which it competes (Porter, 1985). Similar to Bain structure-conduct-performance (SCP) paradigm, the five forces of industry affect the overall industry performance, and thus the performance of firms within the industry.

For the firm's conduct (C), Porter (1980) does place special emphasis particularly with respect to strategy development and strategic choice within the framework of industry structure, which his known as 'generic strategies'. Porter (1980) argues that firms must choose among three generic strategies: 1) low cost leadership; 2) differentiation; and 3) cost or differentiation focus. Each of these strategies represents a fundamentally different means of how firms can compete. There is a linkage between the generic strategies and the value-chain analysis. Porter (1985) developed a comprehensive value-chain analysis and study how these positions were generated within the company and its relationship with the suppliers and buyers. The value-chain is a chain of activities of a firm within a specific industry and firm's competitiveness advantage is developed based on how firm organise and perform its separate activities along the value-chain.

Porter (1985) classified the firm's activities into two types. First activities were classed as "primary activities" and it include the business function such as inbound logistics, operations (production), outbound logistics, marketing and sales (demand), and services (maintenance). The second activities were classed as "support activities" which include administrative infrastructure management, human resource management, technology (R&D), and procurement.

Porter's work represents one of the most widely discussed theoretical foundations for explaining the performance variance among firms in the strategic management literature. His frameworks is clearly influenced by Bain-type I/O economics. In Porter's theory, for example, industry structure is neither viewed as entirely exogenous nor stable, unlike the view in I/O theory (Bain, 1991). Porter (1985) views the external environment as partly subject to the influences of firm actions. He stated that:

"A firm is usually not a prisoner of its industry structure. Firms, through their strategies, can influence the five forces... If a firm can shape structure, it can fundamentally change an industry's attractiveness for better or worse."

In his book *'What is Strategy'* published in 1996, Porter highlighted that strategy is about how firm increase its operational efficiency and effectiveness as well as being able to position itself at the best strategic positioning in the market. Firm's superior performance lies in the ability of a firm to find the new ways of competing and inventing better ways of doing something. This is where the important concept of innovation lies and it is generates from the R & D activities.

a. **Relationship of port resources and performance – The Application of New Organization perspective**

When applying this concept in the port context, Magala (2004) argued that having an excellent port infrastructure and facilities is not enough to gain higher performance. Higher performance can be achieved by differentiating its product and services in a different, efficient and innovative way. Towards the end, what is so important to be competitive is not about the port effectiveness to produce port services but how good the port is in meeting the demand of the shippers by offering the competitive value-added services to the shippers.

Other NIO theory applied by port researchers is the Porter's generic strategies. Most of the scholars agreed that by focusing on the cost leadership and service differentiation strategy, ports would be able to gain a competitive advantage. Haezendonck and Notteboom (2002) demonstrated that ports may gain a competitive advantage by focusing on the niche for port services such as hinterland accessibility, productivity, quality of services, cargo generating effect, port reputation, and reliability of services. Apart from that, Notteboom and Winkelmans (2001) added that the differentiation strategy aims at providing specific services in any market niche distinct from those provided by other ports, thus offering greater value to port users. In contrast, cost leadership strategy, however, implies that ports try to achieve a competitive advantage by becoming low cost provider of port services.

In applying Porter's Diamond model in the seaport industry, Haezendonck, Pison, Rousseeuw, Struyf, and Verbeke (2000) analyse the competitive position of Antwerp by identifying port's strengths and weaknesses as well as examining external threats, opportunities and the current government policy. From the findings, the results showed that locational factor was among important variables of port competitive advantage. They finally revealed that the port benefited from the flexibility and productivity of its dockworkers forwarders as well as port superstructure used but suffered from limited maritime access and low competitiveness of its pilotage and inland navigation service providers.

Another concept of NIO that has been applied in the seaport research is the concept of cluster, which has become the central concept in analysing the competitiveness of nations. Langen (2002) has used the concept of cluster to analyse port competitiveness. He defines seaport cluster as a group of cluster, which consist of business units, public and or private firm which are closely interrelated and functionally linked to the core specialization of the cluster and are located in the proximity of the seaport. Specialization means that port offers highly differentiated services, focus on the customer-driven and value added services. One of the factors that encourage the specialization in the seaport cluster is the nature of the port industry which are closely integrated with the land-based segments in the maritime supply chain (Langen & Pallis, 2007).

Another approach to enhance port competitiveness is applying the value-chain analysis, which has been introduced by Porter (1990). For example Ding (2009b) categorized port capabilities based on the functional activities and value-chain system and the functional activities are classified into primary and supporting activities. As for the primary activities, they include terminal and berth operation system, terminal handling operation system, warehouse and yard system, traffic and marine system, and customer service. As for the supporting activities, they include port infrastructure and general administration affair, human resource management and information technology. They found that the key competency of Kelung Port are creating customer value, quality perception, and IT capability.

2.6.3 Relationship of firm resources and performance based on Revisionist Perspective

The main idea from the Chicago School of Thought in promoting the firm competitiveness is to uphold efficiency in production and distribution. Within this view, firm competitiveness is determined by efficiency gains. In other words, a firm will grow if it can achieve and preserve productive and distributive efficiencies. However, a firm would only be able to achieved efficiency when the firm is capable of producing and selling more than their inefficient competitors. Similarly, a firm will not survive as the competition erodes this source of competitive advantage.

One of the scholar from this school,Stigler (1966) also rejects the view that monopoly incentives and collusive arrangements are central to profit maximization. For the school, monopoly incentives and collusive arrangements are temporary market anomalies, which cannot be sustained in the long-run because the costs of monitoring and enforcing such agreements are prohibitive. Consequently, the profits, if persistent, can only be justified on efficiency grounds.

Barros and Athanassiou (2004) introduced two theoretical models in explaining the variation the firm efficiency within an industry. The first type is based on the strategic-group theory which explains differences of efficiency among firms in a group which is due to the structural characteristic of units within an industry (Caves & Porter, 1977). This in turn, will lead to the differences in firm's performance. The second model, which was adapted, based on Resource-Based View which explains that the different efficiency score among firms is due to the differences in firm resources and skills (Barney, 1991; Rumelt & Teece, 1994; Wernerfelt, 1984).

However, Porter (1980) suggested that firm efficiency can be best applied by using cost leadership strategy. This strategy assessed firm efficiency by dividing firm's resources into five categories which are namely: i) factor input that includes low cost; material, labour productivity, capital to sustain and necessary investment; ii) efficient scale facilities; iii) process engineering skills, minimal wastage or high yields, employee productivity and logistics; iv) product of services which include easily manufactured and capital intensity, and; v) distribution factor which includes efficient scale customers, simple product line and price discrimination.

a. **Relationship of port resources and performance -The application of Revisionist Perspective**

Based from the previous port studies, port efficiency is one of the major determinants of port competitiveness. Port efficiency becomes one of the important factors of port competitiveness, as it will determine the overall shipping cost and port profitability. According to Van de Voorde (2005), port will be able to reduce 12 per cent of total shipping cost if they can improve 25 – 75 per cent port efficiency. It shows that port efficiency act as a major role in determining port of choice among port users particularly the shipping companies.

Among the studies of port efficiency, scholar gave more focused on effective use of terminal and berthing facilities. This is because the optimization of terminal is crucial to ensure that port have higher productivity. High productivity means low waiting time of ship to load and upload their cargo and thus will attract more cargoes and thus port able to achieve higher performance. Tongzon and Ganesalingam (1994) who have measured efficiency of port operation based on capital and labour productivity, asset utilization rate, and customer-oriented measures. Later, Peters (2001) and Tongzon (2005)measured port operational efficiency based on the speed of the container handling and vessel turnaround time.

According to Yang et al., (2011), port resources such as provision of up-to-date facilities and equipment, adequate information technology and port infrastructure play a crucial role in improving overall port efficiency. They stated that other significant determinant affecting port efficiency included the role of Electronic Data Interchange, port handling equipment, such as crane, size of container yard, number of specialized terminal, number of reefer points, number or length of berth, backup space on terminal, super infrastructure and size of port terminal capacity.

Beside port efficiency, other important determinants that contribute to port competitiveness is port effectiveness. According to Magala (2004), in order to achieve the overall port performance and sustain growth, port managers must know that port should not only be efficient, but also be effective. Port effectiveness is determined based on how much business that port could capture. Capturing market opportunities is very crucial and one of the example of competitive strategy which is focused on meeting and delivering the needs and benefits of the shippers. By doing this, ports would be able to retain and sustain competitive advantage over their rivals. The market focused strategies can be effectively achieved if ports have the capabilities and core competency (Magala, 2004).

2.6.4 Relationship of firm resources and performance based on Austrian School of Economics Perspective

The emergence of Austrian School of Economics is to emphasize the roles of entrepreneur and innovation as a basic to firm success. One of the contributions of this school is the introduction of the entrepreneurial theory by Schumpeter (1934). This theory explains that firm will gain competitive advantage if they continuously produce new products and services or new ideas of production process or new ways or techniques of organizing firms. Later Schumpeter (1950) posited the ideas of endogenous technological innovation and *creative destruction* as central to capitalism. This term means that a firms could achieve higher performance if they continuously creating and adopting innovations that would allow them to gain advantage from the market opportunities.

Some innovation is scientific in nature and it growth of innovation is through the process of research and development (R & D) of a firm. Schumpeter (1942) stressed the significant role of R & D in determining the success and competitiveness of a business or firm. In Schumpeter's view, the purpose of firms is to grab opportunities by creating or adapting innovation that make rivals' position obsolete and this kind of competition is much more effective compared to price competition over existing products.

According to Solow (1957), firm's innovation can be in a form of technological advancement and most importantly it need to continuously change through the advancement of knowledge as it is the primary determinant of economic growth. It is supported by Hayes and Abernathy (1980) who confirmed that the key success factor in most industries is the organizational commitment to compete in the market place and it is based on the technological ground. With the advancement of knowledge firm could continuously have short term and long term activities to discover new form of firm's innovation. By discovering new form of innovation, firm could sustain competitive advantage as their rivals could not duplicate or imitate their actions. Thus, for the firm survival, firm should continuously improve their own innovation to gain the better competitive position among rivals.

The valuable contribution of Schumpeter's idea of firm's innovation is the understanding on how port can gain competitive advantage through the mechanism of entrepreneurship and innovation. It is pointed that the power of innovation of a firm is the capability to increase the market power and position of the firm. However, firm's innovation can be a form of technological innovation, managerial strategies, vision, organisational structures and marketing, new ways of handling products or services and new ways of production.

a. **Relationship of port resources and performance- The Application of Austrian School of Economic Perspective**

In the context of seaport studies, shipping and port development were key enablers of the globalization process. The growth and development of shipping and port industry are driven by the technology which from the process of innovation and R&D. According to Blanco et al. (2010), innovation in the sea transportation industry is essential due to the increase of international transaction and freight. Thus, the role of innovation is essential in improving the port efficiency, increases the capacity and speed of the movement of goods and to reduce the unit costs of transport.

There are many examples of the roles of innovation ranging from the innovation of transferring or handling of cargoes, construction of port infrastructure and superstructure including terminal, logistic activity zones and dry port, and IT innovation in management and documentation. Blanco et al. (2010) described that port technological innovation includes: 1) the construction of new infrastructure including terminal, logistic activity zones; 2) the provision of new equipment such as cranes of greater tonnage capacity and specialization, and conveyors; 3) the creation on telematics platforms, which corporate ITC's to streamline document management; and 4) management and organizational changes (introduction of flexible schedules, outsourcing and the involvement of private initiative through administrative concession).

Furthermore, one of the best examples of how technological innovation enhance and sustain port competitiveness is the study on information technology management at PSA Corporation Limited by (2000). They discovered that one of the key management success factors in managing IT to meet the demand and challenges of port operators is the encouragement of IT and creativity. Based on the Austrian School of thought, innovation is a continuous process and therefore a firm should continuously improve its own innovation to gain better competitive position among rivals. Continuous improvement in port innovation needs full participation from various port players such as port authority, terminal operators, shipping companies and other players in the maritime logistic chain. One of the examples is the financial incentive given by Singapore Maritime Division for the shipping industry to encourage port research and development as well as to strengthen the maritime business in the region (Mc Kinnon, 2011). As a result, PSA Corporation Limited has become the world's busiest container port over the last few years.

According to Burroughs (2005), port innovation can be in a form of port techniques, port technology and also port strategies. Examples of port strategies included port's product or process innovation, port's innovation in marketing, logistics and cooperation and integration with other strategic alliances. In addition, as highlighted by Yap and Lam (2006a), port innovation in can be improved by cooperating with other ports or other strategic partners. By having strategic partners port would be able to gain advantage of the resources and technology transfer and this is one of the better ways of competing (Hwang & Chiang, 2010).

2.6.5 Relationship of firm resources and performance based on Profit Impact of Market Share Perspective

Another important strategy for port and firm to sustain in the market is the strategy that focuses on market the market share. According to Buzzell (1975), the important of this strategies lies from its direct causal relationship between market share and profitability of a firm. That is why market share strategy becoming one of the popular in almost every industry specifically in the port sector. It is assumed that by gaining higher market share, firms are able to gain higher profit and maintain superior performance.

Henderson (1979) for example, states, " *in a competitive business, market share determines relative profitability*". The rationales most commonly given to explain the association are that higher market share enables firms to utilize economies of scale/scope to reduce costs and gives firms market power that can used to extract favourable concessions from channel members and customers (Jacobson & Aaker, 1985). In line with this, they offer an explanation on the linking of market share with profitability. He stated that customers use share as a signal of product quality. He agrees that high market share brands represent the high level of product quality and performance and this will increase the higher confidence level among customers as compared to low market share brands (Jacobson & Aaker, 1985).

Buzzell (1975) categorized the market-based strategy into three groups. The first group of this strategy is the strategy based on the new product development and generating new marketing activities. If the market share of a business falls under the lowest point, it usually has two strategic options, which are either to raise part or withdraw. The second one is the defence strategies designed to keep the status quo of the existing condition of the market share represented by a question: 'what is the most profitable way to maintain its market?' The third one is harvest strategies designed to to gain the profit and market share in a short-term period.

One of the major tool used to operationalize such strategies is using the growth-share matrix or other name is 'Boston Box' (Kotler, 1994). This matrix views that firm success and growth lies from the percentage of growth rate prevailing in the market and the relative market share that firm can grasp. Similarly, the centre argument of this strategy is the ability of the firm to the capture higher market share relative to the its rivals in the market (Magala, 2004). However some of the managers that have used this tool argued that market with high growth are more attractive as compared to the declining markets because it propose large chance for firm's growth (Aaker, 1986).

a. **Relationship of firm resources and performance- The Application of PIMS**

In applying the market share focus strategy to determine the competitiveness of firm in port industry, (Magala, 2004) argued that ports would be able to sustain and achieve high market share if they invest in the high growth market such as container trades industry. This is because such market is easier to gain higher market share and has more opportunities to create a new business to the ports.

It is therefore, creating new market, which does not have competitors, is one of the important strategies for the firm's growth. The new market is called the blue ocean strategy whereas entering the existing market is termed as the red ocean strategy. Entering into a new market gives more impact as compared to the existing one (Kim & Mauborgne, 2005). In contrast with the view of the importance of market share, other views attempt to deny that the existing market share will be able to create firm competitive advantage. To them, how customers perceive the product quality is an important indicator for a competitive advantage (Jacobson, 1987). Porter (1980) advanced the counterargument that a high quality image often requires a perception of exclusivity that is incompatible with high market share. He added that increases in the share may diminish the feeling of exclusivity that enhances quality perception.

Firms, which are categorised under low market share businesses, are also able to compete successfully and gain high profit. Kotler (1994) argued that firms in the low share market can compete successfully with their rivals when if they focus on the niches and differentiated product or services. However, before firms can come out with this strategy, they must conduct the research and development activities as a basis for innovation.

In addition, for the low share market segment, firm must possess their own focused services or products where their strengths are highly valued by their customers. This will avoid intense competition by the larger competitors. However, this strategy requires such firms to spend time finding and exploiting valuable opportunities from their own market segment. Firms, which have small market share, are also able to gain high performance as long as that they can focus on the certain market niche. By focusing on the niche market, it would be a significant advantage to the small firms to sustain in the market. Hamel and Prahalad (1994) suggested that the new measures of market influence and profitability need to be extended outside traditional measure which is to include measure of opportunity share. This is because regardless of whether the market growth rate and relative market share are higher or lower, some of the firms are more profitable than others.

2.6.6 Relationship of firm resources and performance based on Resource Based View Perspective.

In the 1970 and 1980, the thinking of strategic management scholars are heavily influenced by the traditional IO economic (Hoskisson et al., 1999). They emphasized on the importance of industry structure towards firm's success. Thus, the attractiveness of the industry is based on the external constraint imposed by the industry structure. However, the industry structure paradigm cannot be expected to provide all answer as to why some firms are more successful than others. Thus, the strategic management scholars began to find the factors inside the firm to understand the performance variability among firms.

Theoretically, the views from RBV continue to explain the sources of firm competitive advantage but narrowing at the firm level. The early concept of RBV can be traced from the important seminal Edith Penrose in the late fifty's. The concept of firm's competitiveness, growth and the main sources of firm competitive advantage were discussed in detailed in her paper "The Growth of the Firm". As a firm always competes for success and profitability, it should exploit its existing resources and at the same creates and develops a new one. She emphasized that, firms may achieve rents not because it has better resources, but rather because the firm's distinctive competence involves making better use of its resources (Mahoney & Pandian, 1992; Penrose, 1959a). According to Penrose (1959a), firm growth is related to the resources under control and the administration framework used to coordinate resource use. The interaction and monitoring resources between firms is thus made difficult, denying rivals the chance of replication, and resource inimitability secures and protects superior returns.

After Penrose (1959a), the concept of the firm resources is discussed and expended by few important scholars especially by those in the strategic management area. The debate on the contribution of the firm resources towards firm performance shows that the firm's internal and external resources have its own characteristics and dimensions. Strategic management scholars tend to define firm resources from many angles.

One of the explanations of this group came from the perspective of firm's production. Taking the Penrose's idea, scholars in this group emphasized on the importance of firm's resources to firm's production process. As pointed out by Wernerfelt (1984), the firm performance is driven by its production and production is actually driven by its resources. This argument is similar to Rubin (1973) who conceptualized firm resources as a bundle of resources that should be processed to make them useful and to gain higher profit. In short, firms should be able to identify and acquire these resources to enable them to success.

The argument and the ideas on the concept of competitive advantage continued with more empirical and testable theoretical framework in RBV. The concept of firm competitive advantage has been viewed similarly with the idea from industrial organization. Two main arguments are related to the differences and the characteristic of the firm resources. Barney (1991) perceived that the resources and capabilities are heterogeneously distributed among firms and imperfectly mobile. These differences must exist and persist overtime, which allows firms to gain competitive advantage. He added that if these resources and capabilities have the criteria of valuable and rare resources, a firm would attain a competitive advantage and enjoy an improved performance in a short term (Barney, 1991). He continued to argue that in order for a firm to sustain these advantage overtime, its resources and capabilities must be inimitable and non-substitutable (Barney, 1991; Dierickx & Cool, 1989). Therefore, there are four main characteristics of resources that have been emphasized to achieve firm competitiveness. These characteristics are valuable, rareness, inimitable and non-substitutable.

In explaining valuable resources, the most important point to be highlighted is the ability of the firm resources to improve firm's efficiency and effectiveness in its operation. In other words, a bundle of resources that a firm accumulates to execute a given market strategy must be more valuable relative to the rest of the competitors in the market. According to Barney (1991), resources are valuable when they help to improve firm efficiency and this is done by satisfying customer needs at the lower cost than competitors.

The second criterion, which is the rare resources, gives the meaning that the resources are only possessed by firms in a particular industry. It is a function of the number of other firms in the competitive arena holding the same resources. If a large number of firms possessed the same resources (even it is valuable), the resources' ability to generate a competitive advantage would be diminished. As pointed out by Barney (1991), the resources are rare if they are possessed by a small number of current competitors or, ideally only one firm.

According to Barney (1991), valuable and rare resources provide opportunities to gain a competitive advantage. However, for a firm to be in a position to exploit valuable and rare resources, there must be resources position barrier to prevent other competitors from imitating those resources. Resources that that valuable and rare could enhance the firm opportunities to gain competitive advantage to the extent that resources are considered very difficult to the rivals to imitate or duplicate. Among the characteristics of resources that cannot be imitate are: 1) must have special historical conditions; 2) must have a causal ambiguous relationship between the resources and 3) must have social complexity of the resources and this means that the social linkages among the resources are difficult to be understood by the competitors (Dierickx & Cool, 1989).

In addition to the explained criteria, Barney (1997) expanded her thought on the sources of competitive advantage by introducing the concept *'organized firm'*. Some examples of the characteristics of the organised firms are: 1) a firm that has a good company's reporting structure; 2) good management control systems; 3) offer the outstanding human resources policies such as compensation and other incentive policies and training; 4) firm's culture. These components of organized firm are also known as complimentary for firm's capabilities and resources. They cannot stand-alone but must be combined with other firm's capabilities. However, having these all components may lead firm able to exploit the full potential of its resources and could sustain a competitive advantage.

Another Stream in Resource-Based View

There are other few arguments and perspectives within the RBV, which contradict with Barney (1991) views. Barney views that firms that owned resources and capabilities that were valuable, rare, non-substitutable, in-imitable and organized firm would attain a competitive advantage. Nevertheless, few scholars argued the reason of firm competitiveness is not its resource possession but more because of its resources exploitation. Thus, the better name for resources was named as 'distinctive competence'. It was referred as the activities that customers recognize as firm's competency which differentiate a firm from its competitors and that therefore provide a competitive advantage. Thus, they argued that firm may achieve rents based on its distinctive competence involvement. Hence, they make a better use of their resources (Mahoney & Pandian, 1992). They continued by suggesting that firms that make the best use of their resources are those that allocate them in such a way that their productivity and /or financial yield are maximized.

i. **Capabilities School**

Various streams of discussion have emerged in the last decade that share a common viewpoint of resources as sources of competitive advantage. The first stream is name as the Capability School. Early researchers in the capabilities school sought to explore if technology, or R & D development, capabilities could provide growth in firm size, markets and industries. For example, Teece (1988), explores the implications of in-house versus contract R&D. He argues that the expansion and growth of firm namely through diversification is driven by the R&D capabilities within the firm. In the 1980, few scholars posit that corporate growth and expansion is an endogenous technological imperative, in which the R&D capabilities of firms largely determine the degree and level of their innovation in product market (Kay, 1988; Lee & Wilde, 1980).

The expansion of the capability school shift to the new concept at the in the nineties which is called Dynamic Capabilities. Scholars from this group proposed that the firm capabilities are always changing and very dynamic in nature. Thus, the core of a dynamic capability is the firm ability to sense and adapt to ever-changing competitive environment through the integration and continuous re-configuration of organizational skills, assets, and functional competencies (Eisenhardt, 2000).

Dynamic capabilities are also been described by Day (1994) as the complex bundles of knowledge within the organisation that allow firms to coordinate and utilize their resources and capabilities to gain higher profit. Some of the example of the dynamic capabilities are new product development, service delivery and order fulfilment.

Other view of dynamic capability is by Collis (1994) which divided capabilities into three folds, first functional activities of a firm such as plant layout and distribution logistic. Second, those activities that allow the firm to learn and adapt changing environmental condition over time. Lastly, the third activity is recognized to have an intrinsic value that can develop firm strategies over competitors. However, Nelson and Winter (1982) explain that firms can generate values and competitive advantage through the notion of routine. He defined routine as "all regular and predictable behavioural pattern of firms" and posits that routine are the core services with which the firm generate value from a firm's factor stocks. This is being achieved through the application of organizational know-how and skills.

Nevertheless, scholars also suggest that some of the dynamic capability is contributing to the competitive advantage. Some capabilities will perform adequately and others will be performed poorly. However, few capabilities must be performed with superiority in order to win competitive advantage over competitor. Thus, Day (1994) argues that firm must have distinctive capabilities to achieve superior levels of success in competitive markets.

ii. **Core Competency School**

A new dimension or perspective of firm competitiveness began to inspire the business world in the early nineties by the introduction of the concept 'core competence'. Instead of using resources as a term, scholars are trying to replace with the term 'competencies'. The important turning point within capability-based school was in 1990 when Prahalad and Hamel (1990) published their 'Core Competence of the Corporation'. Core competencies are firm's capabilities that are crucial to achieve competitive advantage. Firms may develop key areas of expertise, which are distinctive to that firm and also important to firm's long term growth. As argued by Prahalad and Hamel (1990) as " the task of management was to create radical new products, which was enabled by the exploitative nature of firm's core competencies". Much like Penrose (1959a) and Rubin (1973), these authors focused not only on the static resources but also firm's inimitable skills, technologies, knowledge and so forth with which they are deployed. Usually competence activities important at a firm's corporate level which are key to the firm's survival and are central to its strategy.

Additionally, for the firm success, the competencies of a firm must have three main characteristic namely: i) the competencies must able to make a substantial impact to the perceived benefits of the end product or services; ii) should be imperfectly imitable; and iii) should provide an access to a wide variety of markets (Hamel & Prahalad, 1994; Prahalad & Hamel, 1990). The first characteristic of a core competency is perceived customer benefit, which has been stated by Hamel as 'a core competency', which could the products and services to the customer. Thus, core competency is a skill which firms leverage to deliver fundamental customer benefit. This argument is parallel with the Barney's idea on the criteria of valuable resources. Hamel and Prahalad (1994) however argues that the core competencies do not always contribute significantly to customer values but also can give substantial cost benefits to producers.

Instead of that, Hamel also agreed on the concept of in-limitability proposed by Barney (1991). This comes the concept of inimitable of core competency which is define as its ability to resist imitation or completely distinctive or unique as compared to competitors (Hamel & Prahalad, 1994). Other scholar also can view inimitability as an 'isolating mechanism'. One example is in a form of legal protection (Hall, 1992). Legal protection may avoid competitors from easily copying a core competency (Dierickx & Cool, 1989).

The third characteristic of core competency is its ability to provide a channel to enter new market. Firms, which possessed the core competencies, are always creative and innovative in producing new ideas and introducing new products to its new market. This is supported by Hamel and Prahalad (1994)who explained that "core competencies are the gateways to new products". Example of the creative company is Sharp's core competency in designing and developing flat-screen displays has served as a channel to enter a variety of product markets such as camcorders, laptop computers, video projection screen, and pocket television.

iii. **Knowledge-Based Theory (KBT)**

Another stream in the resources-based view family is the knowledge-based theory (KBT) of the firm. This stream emphasized knowledge as the most important and strategic resources to a firm to achieve competitive advantage (Nonaka & Takeuchi, 1995). This is because the nature of knowledge is usually difficult to be imitated, socially complex and it is considered as valuable resources of a firm. Firm who possessed a wide variety of knowledge or know-how among are considered to have more advantage and potential to achieve superior corporate performance and sustained competitive advantage (Grant, 1996; William, 1992).

Researches on KBT are growing in the literature and various forms of knowledge-related thinking are also evolving. For example, Smith (1996) has focused on the intellectual capital which is largely based on the knowledge assets of the firm. Other scholars focused on the issue of knowledge management (Rogers, 1996; Spender & Grant, 1996) while others focused on the emerging structure of the organizational network (Kogut, 2000) information technologies (Alavi & Leidner, 2001).

a. **Relationship of firm resources and performance – The Application of RBV.**

There are only few studies on port competitiveness that have applied the various streams of Resource-Based View. Traditionally, port competitiveness is viewed as how a port increases its performance and it is measured based on port efficiency or productivity. However, the result only shows the relative relationship of both input and output but does not provide the best answer on why do firms better than others and able to sustain competitive advantage of a port. However, the ideas from RBV on how firm should compete among rivals have shed the light on port competitiveness studies and bring up a new perspective on port competitiveness.

Many researchers that have applied the RBV framework in the context of port industry have tried to understand the kind of competence that a port should possess in order to compete successfully against its rivals. Notteboom and Winkelmans (2001) had argued that the analysis on port efficiency and productivity is not enough to measure port competitiveness. In the search of core competencies of a port, they proposed a complete strategic planning for a port based on RBV approach. This strategic planning is important for the port operators and port authority to identify and understand the portfolio of their resources and core competencies in order to achieve port competitive advantage.

There are other examples of port related studies that emphasized on the importance of analysing ports based on port's core competencies. Among the studies included, for example a study on how to achieve competitive advantage, which emphasized on the important of hinterland and distribution capabilities. For example, Haezendonck and Notteboom (2002) argued that port would be able to achieve competitive advantage if its hinterland and distribution capabilities are surrounded in highly competent supply chains and intermodal arrangements, greater access to markets and also has excellent coordination of network among the maritime players and market.

According to Magala (2004), the Resource-Based View suggests that port would become more successful in implementing its strategies if they focus on the effective and efficient use of resources. Some of the port's strategic resources could be in term of an efficient logistics and good transport network, skilled labour, efficient handling of cargoes, excellent storage facilities and unique managerial talent. He added that, before selecting what type of strategies to compete among rivals, port should be able to identify and classify their port resources and capabilities. This should include the assessment of resources and capabilities and their potential for sustainable competitive advantage and the appropriateness of their returns. Only after the assessment of port resources, port managers could select a strategy that enables them to exploit effectively the resources relative to external opportunities and competition.

However, after port competitive advantage has been achieved, sustaining it requires the port management to continually erect barriers to competition in order to avoid the loss of advantage created over time. Heterogeneous and immobile resources alone will not guarantee a sustainable competitive advantage. Port sustainability will occur only when rivals find it difficult to both imitate the competitive advantage-generating resources and develop or acquire strategic substitute for them. Thus, it is important to port management to upgrade and enhance their port resources and capabilities and skills and, to find a new better ways to operate more efficient by emphasizing the research and development, and to always seek new innovation to produce better service to its customers.

Gordon et al. (2005) analysed port competitiveness based on the combination of port resources and capabilities. Port resources include the port location and the natural deep harbour whereas port capabilities consist of supporting government policies, foreign direct investment and well thought out operation and information technology.

Another aspect port capabilities have been identified that give an impact to port competitiveness are include customer value, quality perception and port MIS capability(Ding, 2009a), logistic service and innovation capability (Yang C.C., Marlow, & Lu, 2009),government support, port charges, diversify port ownership, port connectivity, good custom services, expand hinterland (Feng et al., 2012), infrastructures, port accessibilities, port operations and information systems (Azevedo & Ferreira, 2008).All of these factors help to create a sustainable competitive advantage for a port.

There are also other previous studies conducted recently which show another new dimension of port capabilities. One of the study conducted by Tang et al. (2011) which confirm that port interactive capability with other counterpart in the same region effect port economies of scale and widen the ability to attract liners(Tang et al., 2011). The recent development of the research on port competitiveness are focusing on port capability to integrate with other members in the supply chain in bringing the value added to the customers. There is an evolution of practices and research from the traditional approach of examining the sea-leg and maritime operation towards focusing on the creation of liner shipping networks, the value delivered to the customer and application of logistics concepts (Panayides, 2006).

This new dimension of capability requires port to increase the level of integration with inland transports, logistic providers, shipping liners via series of vertical and horizontal mergers acquisitions as well as the formation of alliances(Panayides, 2006;Notteboom and Winkelman, 2001;Robinson, 2002,Panayides and Sosng 2009).These evolution lead to the new measure of port performance and competitiveness which by assessing in terms of port contribution to overall combined channel added value in the whole supply chain.

Study on port competitiveness in Malaysia applying RBV framework is very limited. Subhan and Abdul Ghani (2008), conducted a case study on competitiveness of Port of Tanjung Pelepas. They found that the competitiveness of PTP are related to its own unique resources which are categories under two main resources which is internal resources included location infrastructure, accessibility, core competencies and also external resources which is Strait of Malacca as an important maritime route for international trade.

Another study conducted in Malaysia shows that service quality, efficient management, skills workers, work safety, good relationship, modern technology are among important determinant of port competitiveness (Nik Azli, Jagan, Roszita, Nik Muhammad Aslaam, & Saharuddin, 2011).

Previous studies on port competitive advantage show that RBV framework is already being accepted as a comprehensive framework to test the competitiveness of a port. A wide spectrum and horizon of the resources and capabilities have been explored from the previous port literature. The dynamic of the RBV frame workable to explain why some ports able are to achieve and sustain competitive advantage. In order to be successful, ports need to acquire and develop new port competencies and capabilities. They may even need to dismantle the existing ones depending on the market environment in which they compete. The summarization of the main antecedents of competitiveness is summarized in Table 2.1. As competences are dynamic, they change with time, it depending on the market requirement, intensity of competition and the degree of innovation in the market. It is therefore, to achieve and sustain competitive advantage, port should not only be able to assemble a comprehensive list of prescribed competences but to also able to identify the resources and capabilities to take advantage of emerging market opportunities. This includes the ability of port to fulfil the demands or needs of the shipper by generating a value-creating capability through the continuous innovation activities.

From the previous discussion, we have understood that the issues of competitiveness have been widely discussed since the earlier days. It is about how ports utilize their resources, capabilities and competencies to maximize their profitability and expand their market to achieve and sustain their competitive advantage. To ensure ports always a step further than their rivals and capture a new market opportunities, they need to continuously search for new or better ways of doing things and new ways of thinking.

Even though there are many views that have tried to explain how firms compete and achieve competitive advantage, the main idea behind the competitiveness is about how a firm responds to its environment within its industry and how it uses its own resources and capabilities to achieve higher performance and competitiveness. Table 2.2 below shows some of the important tenets of the scholars in the RBV stream. Based on the antecedents, it can be postulated that Resource-Based View is one of the most dynamic view in the strategic management area.

Based on the previous discussion from the five schools of thoughts, major antecedents of firm competitiveness can be best described in Table 2.1.

School of Thought

Contributors

Contribution to the competitiveness concept

Industrial Organization

Bain (1956)

Hunt (1972)

Caves and Porter (1977)

-Firms gain a competitive advantage by practicing monopoly power, barrier to entry, and introducing SCP paradigm.

-Strategic group concept as a basic for analysing firm competitiveness.

New Industrial Organization

Porter (1980,1985)

-Porter's Five Forces model as a tool to assess the industry's attractiveness and facilitates competitor's analysis.

-Porter's generic strategies (low cost leadership, differentiation, and focus)

Revisionist/Chicago School of Economic
Stigler (1961,1968)
Demsetz (1973)
-Firm is a combination of heterogeneous resources
Superior performance attained via efficiency gains
Austrian School of Economic
Schumpeter
(1942)
Solow (1957)
-Role of entrepreneur's to encourage innovation
-Continuous innovation through R&D
Profit Impact of Market Share
Jacobson and Aeker (1985)
Buzzel and Gale (1987)
-Market share is one of the key drivers of firm superior performance.
-The higher market share enables firms to utilize economies of scale to reduce cost and gives market power
Resources Based View (RBV)
(Main contributors)
Additional Streams of RBV
Capability School
Core competency
Knowledge Based Theory (KBT)
Penrose
(1956)
Barney
(1991)
Peteraf (1993)
Teece et al.,(1997)
Eisenhardt and Martin, (2000)
Prahalad and Hamel (1990)
-Resource and capabilities as determinants for competitive advantage
-Firm can sustained competitive advantage if its resources are inimitable, non-substitute, valuable and rare.
-Resources heterogeneity between firms does exist and that the rents attained from such heterogeneity can be sustained

Table 2.1: Major Antecedent of Firm Competitiveness

Table 2.2: Major Antecedents in RBV Stream

SCHOLARS (YEARS)
UNIQUE CONTRIBUTION/CONCEPT INTRODUCED
RESOURCES CRITERIA TO ACHIEVE FIRM'S COMPETITIVE ADVANTAGE
Penrose (1959)
"Growth of the firm" - Firms are consist of collection of resources.
Internal and external resources
Rubin (1973)
Firm as resources bundle
Must be process raw material to make them useful
Wernerfelt (1984)
Firm's performances are driven directly by its products and it is indirectly driven by resources.
Resources those are critical to development of demanded product.

Hamel and Prahalad (1990)

In order firm to create radical new product, they must exploit firm's core competence

Resources that are "core competence" such as, inimitable skills, technologies and knowledge.

Barney (1991)

Barney (1991),

Dierickx and Cool (1989)

Differences on resources endowment to both exists and persists overtime.

Introducing the resources concept of inimitable and non-substitutable

Resources and capabilities that are heterogeneously distributed and they are imperfectly mobile.

must be valuable and rare can only achieve competitive advantage in a short term.

must be inimitable and non-substitutable to achieve competitive advantage in a long term.

Mahoney and Pandian (1992)

"distinctive capabilities"

firm that can make the best use of their resources are involving the utilization of resources that are productively and financially maximized

Must have distinctive capabilities.

Peteraf (1993)

Henderson and Cockburn (1994)

resources must be properly leveraged and managed

Manageable resources

Barney (1997); Barney and Wright (1998)

Barney and Mackey (2005)

Introduced the concept of "organizational competence" together with the complete framework to assess firm competitiveness named 'VRIO' framework.

expanded the component of organizational competence which includes structure, control system and compensation policies.

Must not only have the characteristics of valuable, rareness, inimitability and non-substitutable but also need to be organized to exploit full potential of firm's resources.

Nonaka and Takeuchi (1995)

Argued that knowledge-based resources are the most relevant to the achievement of a firm's competitive advantages.

Resources must be difficult to duplicate and imitate, socially complex and unique.

Teece Pisano and Shuen (1997)

Expand 'VRIO' framework and highlighted 'dynamic capability' and explained how combination of competence and resources can be developed, deployed and protected

Resources and capabilities or internal and external competence that are build and integrate to address changing environment

Nelson and Winter (1982)

Winter (1995)

Besides other important resources, firm need to possess organizational routine to stay competitive.

Resources that can be coordinated or deployed to replicate 'routines' or webs of relationships.

2.7Empirical evidence on the relationship between port resources and port performance

A study conducted by Feng Ding (2009), using the systematic appraisal model in the Port of Keelung, found the port capabilities such as customer value, quality perception and port MIS capability had positive effect on the port performance.Studies on port competitiveness in Malaysia are very limited.A case study on West Port, Malaysia, using the SWOT analysis showed that the major critical success which included service quality and efficiency, efficient management and good safety management had an impact on port performance(Boonadir, Jagan, Muhammad, & Shaharuddin, 2012).

Subhan and Abdul Ghani (2008) who conducted a case study on the competitiveness of the Port of Tanjung Pelepas in Malaysia found that the higher the level to which resource-based theory of competitive advantage is applied, the higher and longer the growth and competitive advantage would be achieved by this port. This study also compared the resources and capabilities of this port and its rivals. This study also found that this portwas able to compete with its rivals (Port of Singapore, Port Klang and Penang Port) because of its own unique resources that were strategic location, excellence, infrastructure, accessibility and cooperation with other counterparts.

Feng et al. (2012) conducted a large-scale questionnaire survey in two port regions: Western European and Eastern Asian Port. They revealed that government support, port charges, diversified port ownership, port connectivity, good customs services and expanded hinterland had significantly improved port competitiveness and performance.

Yang et. al (2009) examined the relationships between resource, logistics service capability, innovation capability and the performance of Taiwanese container shipping service firms based on the resource-based view (RBV). A structural equation modelling (SEM) approach was employed to test the research hypotheses. The results indicated that port resource had a significant effect on logistics capabilities and innovation capabilities. In addition, the findings indicated that logistics service capability had a positive effect on port performance.

Tang et al. (2011) confirmed that larger ports enjoyed greater direct network effects related to economies of scale, whereas smaller ports leveraged on indirect network effects to widen their scopes of influence to attract vessel calls. Ports tend to engage in more competitive interactions with their counterparts within the same region, even though cooperative relationships among ports across regions are beneficial.

Gordon et al. (2005), used the RBV framework to test the competitiveness of the Port Singapore Authority. The result from the survey interview found that a combination of resources including supportive government policies, ample investment, and well thought out operations and information technology along with location and a natural deep harbour helped to create a sustainable advantage for the Port.

Dai, Xiao, and Cui (2013) used the Structural Equation Modeling to test the data from 30 container ports and 181 responses and results showed that the comprehensive improvement of port logistics capability consists of five dimensions: positioning, integration, infrastructure, operation and agility can directly raise port efficiency and effectiveness performance concurrently. Moreover, via the competitiveness in the market, port logistics capability has an indirect positive impact on port performance.

CHAPTER THREE: THEORETICAL FRAMEWORK OF PORT PERFORMANCE

CHAPTER THREE: THEORETICAL FRAMEWORK OF PORT PERFORMANCE

1. **Introduction**

The objective of this study is to examine the relationship between port tangible and intangible resources and port performance. Therefore, the purpose of this chapter is to construct a framework of port competitiveness based on Resource-Based View model. This model specifically concentrates on the key resources and capabilities, which is crucial on executing strategies in the market.

The early part of this chapter is to explain in brief various theoretical perspectives on firm competitiveness which were discussed previously. These are followed with the justification of selecting resource-based model as the theoretical framework for this study. Following the justification a series of theoretically justified hypotheses are posited.

1. **Industrial Organization and other Management Perspective on Firm Competitiveness**

The objective of this section is to highlight the main ideas of I/O and other five management theories in order to achieve competitive advantage. These theories are namely: Industrial Organisation , New Industrial Organisation, Revisionist View, Revisionist, Austrian School of Economic, Profit Impact of Market Share and Resource-Based View.

3.2.1 Industrial Organization (I/O) Perspective

Industrial organization views that the determinants of firm's performance come from the major source, which is from the firm's industrial structure. I/O argued that there is a relationship between industry structure and firm performance (Mason, 1939). For example, I/O viewed that the key characteristic of the oligopolistic industry structure are materialized in the idea of entry (or exit) barrier (Bain, 1956), and market power is supposed to stem from the presence of structural or behavioural barriers to the entry of new competitors (Porter, 1980).

Bain (1956) operationalized the I/O concept to analyse the industry competitiveness using the model of S-C-P (structure-conduct-performance). SCP paradigm concentrates on the analysis of how the presence of structural or behavioural barriers varies between various industries. In the S-C-P model, the 'S', which stands for the industry structure, is determined by certain attributes such as industry concentration, barrier to entry, number of relative size of firm, existence product differentiation, number of buyers and sellers, the overall elasticity of demand for the industry and vertical integration). Another form of Industry structure can also be in terms of economies of scale and absolute capital requirement, which act as a barrier to entry, which will give an advantage especially for the larger firm. The letter 'C', which stands for conduct, is about the attributes such as pricing behaviour, product strategy and advertising, research and innovation, plant investment and legal tactics. Whereas 'P' stands for performance. It can be in a form of production and efficiency, progress, full employment, and equity.

I/O empirical research provided evidence that a high degree of product differentiation is an important barrier to entry influencing industry profitability differences (Bain, 1956; Bain, 1959; Caves, 1972). Bain (1956) noted that product differentiation of established firms is much more related to heavy advertising activities and sales promotion efforts. Differentiation works to reinforce entry barriers because the cost of overcoming existing customers' buying preferences and loyalties and genuine product differences is too high for the new entrants. Product differentiation refers to the physical or perceptual differences, or enhancements, that make a product special or unique in the eyes of customers.

The I/O view also emphasized the concept of high level of industry concentration, which encourages collusive and monopolistic behaviour among firms (Conner, 1991; Jacobson, 1992). This is believed to allow firms to exercise market power and restrict competition in an industry. In IO views, the existence of firms is to restrain productive output through the collusive agreement that leads to a larger firm and monopoly power. Those firms who have the monopoly power will easily charge for the higher prices and thus will gain higher profitability (Conner, 1991; Jacobson, 1992).

By modifying SCP paradigm, new I/O scholars introduced another new concept which is called 'strategic group'. It is defined as a group of firms in the same industry following similar strategies (Porter, 1980). Firm profitability is regarded as a function of both industry structure and strategic conduct (Cool & Schendel, 1987; Hatten & Schendel, 1977). This concept is similar to the concept of mobility barrier which protects firms in strategic group from entry members of another group. However, strategic group concept is still using the same variables based on SCP paradigm which uses attributes such as scale economies, firm size, product differentiation and distribution network and other SCP attributes as a basis for strategic group formation (Hoskisson et al., 1999).

3.2.2 New Industrial Organization Perspective (NIO)

Strategic management guru, Michael Porter, dominated new Industrial Organization perspective. NIO emphasis firms have an influence on the on the relationship between industry structure and a firm performance (Hansen & Wernerfelt, 1989). This view was clearly specified in his Five Forces Model, which provided a basic analysis for firm and industry competitiveness. His five forces concept was similar to industry structure concept in the SCP model, which was proposed by IO scholars. Like SCP paradigm, the five forces of the industry affect the overall industry performance as well as firm performance within the industry.

Instead of emphasizing the importance of the industry structure and conduct, Porter (1980, 1985) particularly focused on the firm. He argues that firms build and sustain its competitiveness through unique and better competitive strategies than its rivals. These strategies would be used to neutralize competition and make them move to a better position in the market. These strategies can be group into three generic strategies and these include cost leadership strategy, differentiation, or specific market segment.

The cost leadership strategy is strategy, which focused on producing lower cost than the rivals thus firm, will be able to charge lower price and attract higher demand for its products and services. This strategy is dependent firm's ability to utilise the economies of scale and to produce the products and services more efficiently than its competitors are.

Differentiation strategy on the other hand focused on the uniqueness of market and offers higher value to customers as compared to competitors. Firms are able to charge higher prices because their product and services are perceived to have higher quality, features and value. This strategy is able to build barriers to competitors by instilling a sense of loyalty in its consumers. However, differentiation should be is often supported by continuous innovation to make the products or services difficult to imitate by the competitors (Porter 1985).

The third strategy is focusing on the specific segments in which they can compete either as low-cost providers or as providers of differentiated market offerings, or both. According to Porter (1985), competing with one generic strategy is likely to be more successful than competing with two strategies. By focusing only one strategy, it enables firms to utilise the required resources to serve the strategically market segment more efficiently and effectively.

Porter (1985) also related the concept of generic strategies to the firm's value-chain. Firm competitive advantage grows out of the way firms organize and perform its discrete activities, which can be categorized into primary and supported activities.

3.2.3 Revisionist Perspective

Based on the revisionist scholars, firm efficiency has a positive relationship with the firm superior performance and efficiency can be gained through ownership of superior and efficient resource (Demsetz, 1973; Stigler, 1961). A revisionist view emphasized on the firm efficiency as a determinant for firm competitiveness. They also posited that the superior performance can ultimately be explained by the accrual of rent to specialized and high quality resources (Peteraf, 1993).

Based on this school of thought, a firm is a device for changing inputs into outputs. Firm gained efficiency through the maximum utilization of its input which is the firm's resources such as labour, land, capital, management, infrastructure and technological know-how so on so forth. Efficiency is measured by the cost of inputs required to produce a given output. A firm is efficient if it can produce the maximum output with the lower amount of input. Efficient firm is always trying to attain a lower cost possible in its production.

According to Porter (1980), efficient firm is the firm that applied the cost leadership strategy. He states that firm's efficiency can be measured by using several types of firm resources namely factor input that include low cost material, capital to sustain and necessary investment, efficient scale facilities, process engineering skills, employee productivity, efficient logistics, efficient scale customers, labour productivity, simple product line and price discrimination.

3.2.4 Austrian School of Economic

The fourth determinant of firm competitiveness was based on the firm innovation that was emphasized by Schumpeter (1942). He introduced entrepreneurial theories, which discuss the importance of the entrepreneur and innovation as a fundamental for business success. He explained that the central idea of capitalism is from the endogenous technological innovation and creative destruction. He further explained that the firm will grow by constantly creating and adopting innovations that could allow them gain superior advantage than competitors.

In the process of creating and searching for innovation, Schumpeter (1942) emphasized that the research and development (R&D) activities within the firm are important and that these activities should be continuously improved in order for a firm to gain a better position against its rivals (Jacobson, 1992). Firm's innovation could be from the innovation of product, service, device, system, policy or program, that is new to the adopting organization (Daft, 1982).

However, Schumpeter (1942) has categorized innovation into three basic types; i) New products ii) new production processes and iii) new organizational techniques. Later, Damanpour and Gopalakrishnan (2001), classified it into product and process innovation. Product innovation can be defined as a new product or service introduced to meet an external user or market need, while process innovation is defined as a new element introduced in an organization's production or service operations which may include input materials, task specifications and equipment (Utterback & Abernathy, 1975).

3.2.5 Profit Impact of Market Share Perspective

The fifth determinant of firm competitiveness is based on market share, which falls under PIMS view. Buzzell (1975), explained that here is a causal relationship between market share and firm profitability. Market share is considered the major attribute in determining firm success due to the reason that market share enables firms to utilize the economies of scale to reduce cost (Jacobson & Aaker, 1985).

According to Hellofs and Jacobson (1999), customers use market share as a symbol for product quality. Therefore, firms who have higher market share are able to charge higher price and definitely will get higher return as compared to low market share firms. In contrast, few scholars give different views proposing that firms who have low market share are able to achieve high return and profit if they focus on the market niche or differentiated market. They argued that lower market share firms would achieve high performance if they efficiently use its research and development activities for the basis of firm innovation (Hall, 1992; Kotler, 1994).

3.2.6 Resource-Based View Perspective

The resource-based view emphasized the importance of firm resources which have the characteristic of heterogeneous, imperfectly mobile and unique in creating and sustaining a competitive advantage (Photis & Gray, 1999). For a firm to gain higher performance and sustain competitive advantage, it must possess such strategic resources that are valuable, rare, imperfectly imitable and difficult to substitute (Barney,1991).

The RBV theory defines firm resources as *"all assets, capabilities, organizational process, firm attributes, information, knowledge, etc. controlled by firm"* (Barney, 1991, p.101), and proposes that a firm has a competitive advantage when it creates a successful strategy based on firm resources that cannot be duplicated by competitors. There are few scholars who contributed to the Resources-Based theory. These scholars can be grouped into three major streams. The first stream is capabilities school which focuses on the importance of technology and R&D development as a main determinant for firm and market growth. Teece (1988) posited that the competitiveness of a firm is the result of its R&D capabilities as well as its level of technological innovation. The concept of capabilities was shifted to dynamic capabilities. The idea of dynamic capability is that the firm should be able to adapt to ever-changing competitive environment through the integration and re-configuration of organizational skills, assets, and functional competencies (Teece and Shuen, 1997).

The second stream within the RBV school is highlighting the concept of core competency that was popularized by Prahalad and Hamel (1990) who emphasized on the uniqueness of resources endowment. The uniqueness of the firm resources are based on three major characteristics. First, firm resources should make a significant contribution to the perceived customer benefits of the end of the product. Second, they should be imperfectly inimitable. Finally, they should provide a gateway to a wide variety of market (Hamel & Prahalad, 1994; Prahalad & Hamel, 1990).

The third stream under the RBV School is based on knowledge-based theory (KBT). This theory posits that knowledge, or know-how is the primary source which explains why a firm performs better than others (Grant, 1996; William, 1992). Firms that have the knowledge capability are able to create and share the knowledge and this will give them a distinctive competency over other institutional arrangement such as market (Nahapiet & Ghoshal, 1998).

3.3 The application of firm competitiveness theory in port related studies

As a firm, a port also applies various theories of firm competitiveness as discussed in the earlier chapter. However, based on many theories of firm competitiveness, there are only few theories that have been applied in port industry. Table 3.1 below shows a number of research studies, which are related to the area of port competitiveness, based on past and recent literature.

Table 3.1: The Application of Firm's Competitiveness Theory in Port Related Studies

Theory of firm competitiveness

Port competitiveness related studies

Authors/years

Topics of interest

Industrial Organization
Langen and Pallis (2007)
Langen (2004)
Huybrecths et al., (2002)
Oliver (2003)
Oliver (2005)
Applying the concept of entry barriers
Analysing performance of seaport cluster
Applying port strategic group between port ship-owner, logistic providers and shippers
Ocean carriers entry strategies to enter port sector
Private entry and partnership and in container terminal
New Industrial Organisation
Manual A Costa et al.,2007
Haezendonck et al, (2000)
World Bank (2001)
Yap and Lam (2006)
Zauner (2008)
Analysis of port using extended Porter's Diamond
Applying Porter's Diamond identifying strengths and weaknesses of seaport cluster
Promoting liberal reforms through various development strategies using Porter's model
Using Porter's framework to address changes and competition in European port
Applying Porter's Diamond to analyse container transhipment hub in Southeast Asia.
Revisionist
Cullinane et al., (2006)
Tongzon and Gunasingalam(1994)
Peter (2001)
Tongzon and Heng (2005)
Tongzon (1989)
Barros and Managi (2008)
Applying DEA and Stochastic Cobb-Douglas to analyse technical efficiency of world largest port
Measuring port efficiency based on capital and labour productivity
Port privatization increase efficiency and competitiveness
Port efficiency and international competitiveness
Port efficiency and international competitiveness
Profit Impact of Market Share
Haezendonck (2001)
Yanbing and Zhongzhen (2005)
Song and Yeo (2004)
Applying growth-share analysis as a basic tool determining port competitive position
Determining port competition ability and market share of container port using Analytical Hierarchy Process (AHP)
Analyse Chinese container ports using AHP
Austrian School of Economic
Blanco et al., (2010)
Sihombing(2007)
Perception of Spanish Port Authorities on innovation in the national port system
Resource-based view
Subhan and Abd Ghani (2010)

Emphasized on the port resource that are unique, and resilient core competencies

Based on the past literature on port competitiveness, almost all of the discussions have applied some of the theories of firm competitiveness. For example, a few number of the researches from the Industrial Organisation perspective discussed port strategies to remain competitive by applying the concepts of strategic group and cluster (Langen, 2004), entry strategies (Olivier, 2005), entry barrier (Langen & Pallis, 2007) and vertical integration (Musso et al., 2001). From the perspective of New Industrial Organisation, most of the researches applied Porter's Diamond model to analyse port industry's competitive position and this model is likely popular compared to other models (Huybrechts et al., 2002; Lam & Yap, 2006; World Bank, 2001). Alternatively, Porter's value chain analysis are among the selected model used by port operators and authorities to analyse the competitiveness of ports(De Langen & Van Der Lugt, 2006).

Another important view of port competitiveness is based on the perspective of firm efficiency. In this perspective, port competitiveness can be achieved by emphasizing of technical and operational efficiency especially at the port terminal. Firm efficiency is measured by the efficiency of its inputs over its output. Inputs are basic factors of production such as labour, land, capital, management, and technological expertise. Outputs are the goods and services that the business produces. Holding this concept, this shows the importance of the firm resources in determining firm competitiveness. One of the popular models in measuring port efficiency is using Data Envelopment Analysis (DEA). Some other input in measuring port efficiency is based on manpower, capital, cargo uniformity (Roll & Hayuth, 1993) container throughput (Tongzon & Heng, 2005), price of labour, price of capital, and ships and cargo trend (Barros & Athanassiou, 2004). However, the units of output that are normally used in port studies are cargo throughput, level of service, customer satisfaction, ship calls (Roll & Hayuth, 1993), total cost, terminal quay length, numbers of quay cranes, and port size (Tongzon & Heng, 2005).

The theory of firm efficiency cannot be separated from the theory of firm innovation. In order to be efficient, firms need the advancement of technology, which resulted from the innovation and R&D activities in firms. Firm's innovation refers to the act of creating new products, production processes, and organizational techniques (Schumpeter, 1934, 1942). In creating innovation, firms need the resources, skills, and capabilities. This also shows the importance of firm resources in determining firm competitiveness. As port industry has to face the increasing pressure due to globalization and trade, the theory of innovation is based on (Schumpeter, 1934)has made a huge contribution to the development of port strategy. Among port innovation in the port industry such as terminal and technological innovation, provision of new and equipment, innovation in port safety and security, environmental and quality, innovation in management and organization change(Sihombing, 2007).

Other firm competitiveness theories which have also been given priority in port industry are based on the Profit Impact of Market Share (PIMS). However, the past researches, which focused on the strategy of market share impact on the port competitiveness, are very limited. Among the important tools in analysing market share in port industry was based on growth-share metric (Haezendonck & Notteboom, 2002) and Analytical Hierarchy Process (Song & Yeo, 2004; Yanbing, Zhongzhen, Zan, & Zhi, 2005).

Finally, After the 1990 the researches based on port competitiveness studies have also been dominated by the Resource-Based Perspective. Some of the previous researches which have applied this view are namely: value, rareness, valuable and in-imitable (Azevedo & Ferreira, 2008; Gordon et al., 2005), core competencies (Haezendonck et al., 2000) and port resources and capabilities (Magala, 2004; Pillai, 2006).

3.4 The Justification of Choosing RBV Framework in Analyzing Port Competitiveness

Based on the discussion on the theories of firm competitiveness, generally, there are two main streams of theories. The first is industry-based theories (e.g. the S-C-P paradigm, Porter's Five Forces) which more emphasized the on external industry factors as the principal sources of competitive advantage and rent generation. The second stream was based on the firm based theories (e.g. Resource-Based View, Innovation Theory, Porter's Generic Theory) which are more focused on the right combination of external market in which firm operates and firm internal factors, which are resources and capabilities. The centre argument of RBV is that, internal firm's resources and capabilities are the main sources to achieve competitive advantage than the external factors.

As discussed in the previous sub-chapter written above, there are few theories and models have been used to analyse the port competitiveness and performance. Based from the previous port literature on port competitiveness, the widely accepted approach to analysis the competitive advantage of a port is more focused on the port efficiency which is from the Revisionist school of thought (Barros & Athanassiou, 2004; Cullinane et al., 2005; Tongzon & Heng, 2005). However, the crucial contribution of port resources and capabilities in achieving higher port efficiency cannot be denied. Besides that, the contribution of resources and capabilities has also been extremely significant in enhancing port performance and competitiveness based on the perspective on Austrian School of Thought. This theory has given priority to the importance of firm innovation to enhance the maximum utilization of resources and capabilities to gain higher profit and competitiveness (Blanco et al., 2010; Sihombing, 2007; Woudsma, Hall, & O'Brien, 2009).

Previous studies were also shown that there are many other models that could be used in analysing port competitiveness. Among the most commonly used is the Porter's Diamond Model which was drawn from the New Industrial Organisation School of Thought (Haezendonck & Notteboom, 2002; Huybrechts et al., 2002). However, more recent studies shows that the ideas from Industrial Organisation School of thought are also gain more interest from the port studies scholars. Among the important contributions are the application of the concept of entry barriers, monopoly power, vertical and horizontal integration, strategic group, port cluster and consolidation among ports and other major players in maritime industry (Langen, 2002; Langen & Pallis, 2007; Musso et al., 2001; Olivier, 2005; A. A. Pallis et al., 2008). However, these theories are more focused towards the external factors of a firm (industry structure).

The literature reveals that there is an inclusive empirical evidence for industry structure as the key determinant of firm success. Some of the studies showed that the findings are inconclusive with respect to verifying that industry structure factors are the main determinants of performance variability. Table 3.2 below shows some of the results from the empirical research on the effect of firm level and industry level on firm competitiveness. Most of the results showed that the firm level effect has given more impact on the firm performance as compared to industry level effect. The performance differences within the firm in the industry due to the differences of the attributes of its resources will significantly affect the firm performance.

Thus, to answer why performance differs within the firm in the industry, the theory of firm performance formalized in the Resource-Based View. Therefore, for the purpose of the creation for the research framework, the researcher would choose the RBV perspective to analyse the influence of resources and capabilities among Malaysian ports.

Table 3.2: Empirical Research on the effect of firm level and industry on firm competitiveness

Authors /Years	**Findings**	
	Firm level effect	Industry level effect
(Hansen & Wernerfelt, 1989)	38%	18.5%
(Rumelt, 1991)	46%	4%
(Roquebert, Phillips, & Westfall, 1996)	18%	10%
(McGahan, Anita, & Porter, 1997)		

36%
19%

(Mauri & Michaels, 1998)

25%
6%

(McGahan & Anita, 1999a)

66%
30%

(Hawawini, Subramanian, & Verdin, 2003)

36%
8%

The central model of RBV is to know how a firm exploits its resources in order to gain a sustainable competitive advantage that affords the accrual of superior performance (Barney, 1991; Peteraf, 1993; Wernerfelt, 1984). Drawing on the argument by Penrose (1959), Rumelt (1984) and others, Barney (1991) based his articulation of the RBV on two fundamental assumptions. The first assumption was that, resources and capabilities are heterogeneously distributed among firms. The second assumption is that the resources are imperfectly mobile. He also argued that firms that possess resources that are valuable and rare would attain a competitive advantage and enjoy an improved performance in the short term. In order for firms to sustain the competitive advantage over time, their resources should also be inimitable and non-substitutable.

In the previous RBV literature, researchers, who analysed firm competitive advantage, have come up with various concepts and frameworks. Some of the key concepts of the RBV include concepts such as resources, competences, core competencies, capabilities and dynamic capabilities (Rugman & Verbeke, 2002). These concepts are among the most important concepts and have been widely used by many researchers in RBV studies. These concepts also provide a foundation in building the conceptual framework in analysing firm competitive advantage and performance especially within the empirical research.

According to Newbert (2007), RBV empirical research can be categorized into three different groups. The first group is based on resource heterogeneity approach. The scholars of this group argue on the theoretical ground that a given resource, capability or core competence is valuable, rare, inimitable and or non-substitutable, quantify the amount possessed by a firm, and correlate this amount to some measure of competitive advantage or performance (Barney, 1991; Deephouse, 2000).

The second group employing an organizing approach seek to identify those firm-level conditions that enable effective utilization of resource and capabilities under examination. The organising context is more focus on the execution of skill that will ensure proper resources utilization comprised organisational components such as firm structure, control systems, human resource policy, firm's contract, routine and culture (Barney & Mackey, 2005; Winter, 1995). This approach was considered as a firm level strategy that encourage firm to utilize the right combination of it resources and capabilities and it is also call as dynamic capability approach Teece and Shuen (1997). This approach is trying to test the relationship between firm resources and specific firm dynamic capabilities and firm competitive advantage or performance (Eisenhardt, 2000; Martin et al., 1991; Zhu & Kraemer, 2002).

The third approach is known as conceptual approach and this group is trying to find or test whether the characteristics prescribes by Barney (1991) as crucial for resources and capabilities to contribute to a firm's advantage (King & Zeithaml, 2001). One of the most important characteristic that contribute to firm's competitive position and advantage is the in-imitability. As found by Newbert (2007), the majority of the empirical test (70% of the test) in RBV studies propose that this attribute is among the most important among others.

According to Newbert (2007), among all the three approaches, the organizing and conceptual approach are more important in determining firm competitive advantage as compared resource heterogeneity approach. However, some of the RBV researchers have stated that possession of valuable, rare, inimitable and non-substitute is an essential but insufficient condition for explaining a firm's competitive position (Barney, 1997; Eisenhardt, 2000; Martin et al., 1991). These scholars suggest that a resource can only contribute to this end when it is paired with an appropriate dynamic capability or organizing context. They further suggested that the future research should focus forward either the organizing approach or dynamic capabilities in order to test theoretical model.

Based on the discussion above, it is clear that while empirical research sought to find out the sources of competitive advantage, scholars agreed that there are many others new areas or aspects of research that should be emphasized. However, the loophole of the RBV research using the organising and conceptual approach is needs to be solved.

According to Levitas and Chi (2002), the empirical research on RBV is important because the link between resources and firm success is neither straightforward nor simple, and no single researcher or research study has defined the relationship fully. Instead, different scholars have studied different aspects of connection. As stressed by Andersen and Suat Kheam (1998), the boundaries between the concept of resources, skills and capabilities are not clear. Caloghirou, Kastelli, and Tsakanikas (2004) noted that, *"research on firm-specific assets and capabilities has not reached maturity. Therefore, the existing literature lacks widely accepted and consistent operationalization of the relevant constructs."*

Facing this difficulty, this study attempts to use the concept of organising and dynamic capability approach to examine the relationship between port resources and capabilities in a single industry, which is the port industry in Malaysia. The variables of port capabilities which taken from the organising approach are consist of port structure, control systems, compensation policies, contractual agreement, reputation, culture, human and resources management policies. Other elements of port capabilities are taken from the concept of port dynamic capabilities, which consist of relational ability, routines, employee know-how, and manager know-how.

The next sub-chapter explained in detail the conceptual model of analysing Malaysian port competitiveness using the framework of Resource-Based View.

3.5 The Conceptual Model and Research Hypotheses

For developing a conceptual model for this study, this section is attempts to discuss the relationship between port resources and performance based on the previous findings.. It will be followed by the construct of Resource-Based View model in analysing port competitiveness.

3.6 Theoretical Justification and Research Hypotheses

The main purpose of this study is to empirically test the influence of a variety of resources and capabilities on port performance. Based on the conceptual framework, the following sub-section develops the hypotheses used for this research. The development of the hypotheses is based on the theoretical justification on each of the elements from the proposed theoretical framework.

3.6.1 Port financial asset and Port performance

According to the RBV framework, tangible assets only contribute little to a firm's competitive advantage. Indeed, Amit and Shoemaker (1993) and (Michalisin, Smith, & Kline, 1997), for example, suggested that the resources that drive a firm's performance are the intangibles rather than tangible. Similarly,Soo (2001) suggested that because tangible resources are not valuable, rare, inimitable, or non-substitutable, they are rendered non-strategic to a firm's success.

With regard to firm's financial resources, it is one of the tangible assets and thus is not a source of competitive advantage (Amit Sheoemaker, 1993; Teece, 1998a; Barney, 2001b). This is because financial resources are easily imitated by competitors (Barney, 1991). Itami and Roehl (1987) and Wernerfelt (1989) argued that financial and physical assets have relatively fixed long-run capacity whereas intangible resources have relatively unlimited capacity.

However, port literature provides a different view in which the financial assets are thought to be one of the determinants of a firm financial performance. One of the reasons why it is such is that firms in the port industry need a higher capital to buy new equipment and build new terminal or plant. Port increased capital by getting government loans and by forming vertical and horizontal integration with other shipping lines. To gain an advantage over rivals, financial capital, in a form of debt, may be necessary to expand operations and to realize new growth. Thus, while debt is an asset, it may be an important determinant of market and financial performance (Boulton, Libert, & Samek, 2000). Based from this argument, the research first hypothesis is as follows:

H1: There is a significant relationship between financial assets and port performance.

3.6.2 Port Physical Assets and Port Performance

The literature on the relationship of physical assets and firm performance has produced mixed results. On the one hand, the previous literature on RBV argued that firm physical assets are not a source of competitive advantage, so it cannot increase firm performance. This is based on the nature of physical assets, which are subject to imitation and easily tradable in the market. As argued by previous literature, physical assets do not have the characteristics of value, inimitability, rarity and non-substitutability.

Harvey, Speier, and Novicevic (2001) argue that given the ready availability of financial capital and the rather equal factor endowment of the industrialized nations of the world today, the ease with which they are made makes physical assets relatively more prevalent and less valuable than in the competitive eras of the past.

On the other hand, previous port literature argued that port tangible assets are described as one of the important elements to achieve higher port performance. For example, Haezendock and Notteboom (2002), Malchow and Kanafani (2001)pointed out that hinterland accessibility plays a critical role in strengthening port competitiveness. Since containerisation and liner shipping network involved transferring cargoes around the world, the concept of hub port and transhipment hub act as a transaction centre that served as interfaces for regional distribution network and this needs a good hinterland accessibility (Haynes, 1997). Van Klink and Van der Berg (1998) defined port hinterland as the continental area of origin and destination of traffic flows through a port and they found out that a good hinterland accessibility plays a significant role for enhancing port competitiveness and performance.

In addition, Haezendonck et al. (2000)agreed that port physical assets are important to port performance. They named port physical assets as factor conditions, which consist of production, labour, port infrastructure, good hinterland accessibility, and port location. Without these factors, ports will not be able to attract liners or cargoes and thus reduce port efficiency and competitiveness. Based on the argument above, second hypothesis is as follows:

H2 :There is a significant relationship between physical assets and port performance

3.6.3 Port Technology and Port Performance

The previous literature on the relationship between technology and firm performance also produced mixed results. Based on the RBV perspective, as technology is perceived as one of the tangible assets, this asset is argued to be easily imitated, very easily to find in the market. As a result, it is not a source of firm competitive advantage.

According to Haezendonck and Notteboom (2002) port cannot rely on the technological competencies because the equipment and the system are easily replicated and duplicated by the competitors. The technology its self is being gradually standardised, less durable and easily transferred to other ports. However, technology competencies could make port increase their operational efficiency and thus port will be getting better position in the future. Since port efficiency and productivity are crucially important for port competitiveness, the advancement of port technology and innovation give a major impact to port performance and competitiveness.

In contrast, the previous port literature argued that port technological assets are important to achieve high port performances as they reduce the overall port operation and increase high economies of scale. For example, Gordon et al. (2005) agree that advanced technology in port operation and information technology will increase a sustainable advantage for ports if it is based on the complexity of technologies and skills. The complexity of the technologies and skills would turn into port competencies and will generate higher profitability if it is difficult to be imitated by the competing ports. Based on the argument above, the third hypothesis of this study is as follows:

H3 :There is a significant relationship between technological assets and port performance

3.6.4Intellectual Property Assets and Port Performance

With respect to resources-based advantage, tangible resources are generally viewed not to be a source of competitive advantage (Amit & Shoemaker, 1993; Barney, 1991). There are two main reasons for this argument. First, the tangible resources are easily attained in the markets, thus the profitability will possibly accrue to all firms and offer normal as opposed to higher returns. Second reason is because the tangible resources are subject to being observed and duplicated by the rivals (Barney, 1991).

Strategic management researches agree that one way resources can be protected from competitors duplication is via legal property rights (Hall, 1992). Example of the Intellectual property rights is copyrights, patents, registered design, and or trademark. From the competitiveness perspective, Bosworth (2001) found that patents and trademark are significantly associated with market value of services firms. Other form of intellectual property rights is proprietary (or held-in-secret) technology. Schroeder et al., (2002) argued that firm's proprietary technology have a positive relationship with firm performance.. Based on the argument above, thus the fourth hypothesis is as follow:

H4 :There is a significant relationship between intellectual property assets and port performance.

3.6.5 Organisational Assets and Port Performance

One of the intangible resources assets in a firm is organizational assets. The previous literature showed that organizational assets may also be one of the intangible assets that can exert efforts in resources position barriers and thus resist the duplication efforts of competitors (Edvinsson & Malone, 1997; Fernandez, 2000). One of the examples is the contractual agreements, which are some form of firms' efforts to expand their market through licensing and franchising agreements. Contracts are legally enforceable, thus they may prevent competitors from replicating the economic benefits derived from such agreements.

Another element of organizational assets is culture, which is important for firm success because it defines and underpins the values and behaviours of the firm (Fiol, 2001). The dynamic intersection of firm values and behaviour in turn creates an environment within which the firm's employees can excel. In this sense, a firm organizational culture is a resource that has an impact on its success while at the same difficult for competitors to replicate because of the conditions of assets specificity and time compression diseconomies (Dierickx & Cool, 1989).

Another important element in of organisational assets is the human resource management (HRM) policies (Itami, 1987). According to Huselid (1995) and Lazear (2000), empirical evidence shows that excellent HRM policies could lead to the higher financial and operational performance and competitiveness. Among the HRM policies are recruitment and selection of employee, develop and retain human talent such as training compensation, and recognition programs.

Lastly, organizational structure is also one of the key intangible assets that contribute to the sustainability of a firm's success (Grant, 2002). Organizational structure refers to the division of labour into various tasks within a firm and accountability model from which individuals within the firm are 'mapped' (Mintzberg, 1993). It may serve as one of the important assets, which competitors cannot easily imitate (Boulton et al., 2000).

In the context of port literature, port organizational assets are among the crucial factors strengthening port competitiveness. One of the elements in organizational assets is contractual agreements among port players (port authorities, shipping lines and terminal operators). Since both vertical and horizontal integration of the blue water operations with land-based ICDs (Inland Clearing Deport), railroad and road operation, terminal and freight forwarding or logistic operators have been common, contractual agreements such as strategic alliances, joint venture, merger, and acquisition among port players are becoming crucially important. Alliances and other co-operation are now controlling significant goods flows on the major route on which they are deploying larger vessels (Heaver, Meersman, & Van de Voorde, 2001). These forms of cooperation is to achieve a greater control of the logistic chain (Heaver et al., 2001).

According to Notteboom and Winkelmans (2001), hub status should develop competitive advantages based on unique and resilient core competencies and by forming horizontal and vertical integrations. By forming cooperation, port players can achieve economies of scale and scope and thus will enhance port competitiveness (Yap & Lam, 2006a). Song and Yeo (2004) agreed that in order to cope with changing environment, a certain form of competition and cooperation among ports is necessary in order to provide services that fit into shipping lines' strategies. Based on the above argument, the fifth hypothesis of this study is as follows:

H5 :There is a significant relationship between organisational assets and port performance

3.6.6 Port Capabilities and Port Performance

Previous studies shown that one of the most important sources of firm competitive advantage are from the resources skills and capabilities. These groups of resources are comprised the know-how of employees, the know-how of managers, firm relational ability, and routines. Among these resources, the employee know-how is the main driver of a firm's capabilities and competitiveness because from the employee know-how, they could decide how, when, and where a firm will deploy its other resources (Itami, 1987; Prahalad & Hamel, 1990).

For the managerial perspective, Penrose (1959a) argued that firm's growth is limited only by the abilities and experience, or know-how of its managers. She also suggested that in the struggle for survival in markets, the ability to generate creative innovations, adaptive responses to competitive and environmental factors is contingent upon managerial experience and skill. Coff (1999) argued that the managerial know-how of a manager is one of essential resources for generating a competitive advantage.

Another element of firm capabilities is firm relational ability. Several scholars argued that because firms are not island unto themselves competing alone in impersonal markets, they must effectively build and maintain complex relationship with constituents in external networks, such as alliances and other partners, in order to drive business success. For example, Porter (1990) stated that the ability to create close working relationship with suppliers over time affords a firm access to new information, new ideas, and new innovation—all of which can lead to advantages over rivals.

From a customer perspective, Slater (1997) suggested that the ability to work well with customers, learning about them and from them is essential to a firm's survival. This argument is supported by Powell, Koput, and Smith-Doerr (1996) who stressed that the ability to build and maintain relationships with firm external constituents not only essential for competitive success but it is largely reflective of a knowledge generating, knowledge sharing and learning ability of a firm (Slater, 1997). This relational ability is one of the major sources of firm competitive because it established a socially complex relationship, which cannot be understood by the competitors.

Lastly, another element of firm's capabilities is firm routine, which is the ability of a firm to efficiently transform the inputs into outputs because it requires interactions between management and employees and between personnel and tangible assets (Fahy, 2002). Routines are defined as guiding rules for how work gets completed and how inputs are transformed into outputs Day (1994). Routines are normally codified in a firm's manual and they largely become knowledge-based flows embedded within a firm. It serves as an important guideline of what do's and don'ts (Zollo & Winter, 1999). Based on their nature that is likely to be imperfectly understood by competitors as Zollo and Winter (1999) argue that routines can be among the most critically important sources of firm success.

In sum, firm capabilities are described as the most crucial factors contributing to performance. This is because capabilities are tacit in nature and they are intricately embedded in organizational experience, learning, and practice (Kogut & Zander, 1996). Based from these argument, the firm capabilities are argued to be the most difficult resources to duplicate due to their possessing the highest level of causal ambiguity Teece (2000).

Port capabilities and their relationship with port performance and competitiveness are widely discussed in the port literature. Port capabilities in port operations and technologies have turned into port competencies, which have strengthened port competitiveness as well as port performances (Ding, 2009b; Gordon et al., 2005). Given the discussion above the sixth hypothesis is posited below:

H6 :There is a significant relationship between financial assets and port performance

3.6.7 Port Intangible Assets and Port Performance

Scholars in port studies have different views in determining the major factors contributing to higher port performance. However, the views can be simplified into main groups. The first group is arguing that port tangible resources are more important to achieve port performance. For this study, tangible factors are included port physical resources (strategic location, infrastructure, super-structure), port financial capability, and port technological. The second group is more focused on the important of port intangible resources (port capabilities, skills, relation, reputation and organisational assets, efficiency).

The intangible assets are unlike the physical ones. They are argued to be more difficult to 'build' and thus easily duplicated by the competitors (Amit & Schoemaker, 1993; Barney, 1997). According to Grant (2002), the intangible resources are generally available and can be bought and even transferred from one to another. The scholars would seem to suggest that intangible resources should be more valuable and contribute more significantly to firm success than either financial or physical (tangible) assets. However, based on the Resource-Based View, intangible resources would be a source of competitive advantage if they are namely: i) valuable; ii) rare iii) inimitable; and iv) non-substitutable (Barney, 1991). They are also arguing that the intangible resources are the strategic resources for the firm and thus have an advantage to contribute to higher firm and port performance. Based from these different views, the objectives of this study to identify which resources are more important to port performance. Based on these perspectives, the last hypothesis of this study is posited below:

H7 :Port intangible resources have more influence in achieving higher port performance than port tangible resources

3.7 Proposed Conceptual Framework

Previous literature discusses that there are varieties of resources and capabilities that influence the firm's performance. However, for creating a conceptual model for this study, common categorizations of port resources and capabilities were developed based on the RBV conceptual framework. In this framework, port resources are divided into two main categories, which include port tangible and intangible resources. The dimensions of the tangible resources are namely physical assets, financial assets, and the technological assets. The dimensions of the intangible assets are the intellectual property assets, the organizational assets and port capabilities. The dependent variable for this framework is port performance. There are three dimensions used to measure port performance in this study which are port profitability, volume of cargoes loaded in TEU (twenty foot equivalent units), and volume of cargoes loaded in throughput (tonnage). The proposed conceptual framework for this study is presented in Figure 1.

Tangible Resources

- Physical Assets
- Financial Asset
- Technological Assets

Intangible Resources

- Intellectual Property Assets
- Organizational Assets
- Capabilities

Port Performance

- Profitability
- TEU
- Throughput

Figure 1: Proposed Theoretical Frameworks for Evaluating Malaysian Port Performance

Based on the proposed framework, research hypotheses for this study are as follows:

H1 :There is a significant relationship between financial assets and port performance.

H2 :There is a significant relationship between physical assets and port performance.

H3 :There is a significant relationship between technological assets port and performance.

H4 :There is a significant relationship between intellectual property assets and port performance.

H5 :There is a significant relationship between organisational assets and port performance.

H6 :There is a significant relationship between capabilities and port performance.

H7 :Port intangible resources have more influence in achieving higher port performance than port tangible resources.

CHAPTER FOUR: ANALYSIS OF PORT PERFORMANCE

CHAPTER FOUR: ANALYSIS OF PORT PERFORMANCE

4.1 Introduction

The purpose of this chapter is to explain the empirical findings of the study which was conducted to test the research hypotheses. Firstly this chapter describes overview of the data collection. Secondly, it presents the profile of the respondents. It then follows with descriptive statistic of each variable and analysis on goodness of measures. Finally the results of the hypotheses testing are presented.

4.2 Response Rate

For the data collection purposes, 300 questionnaires were distributed during the self-administered survey. Out of this number, 103 completed questionnaires were returned. A frequency test was run for every variable to screen and clean the data from any missing responses. All 103 completed questionnaires are found to be completed without any missing responses. This made the total response rate for self-administered survey to be 26.6 percent. For the mail-survey, 50 questionnaires were sent but only 20 of completed questionnaires were returned. Thus, the response rate for mail survey was 40 percent. As a result, the total numbers of completed questionnaires from both methods was 123 questionnaires.

4.3 Test of Non-Responses Bias

Non-response bias refers to the differences of the responses between the early and late respondents due to diverse demographic factors such as gender, age, and educational level (Chang and Lee, 2007). For this research, the late respondents were treated as non-respondents (Armstrong & Overton, 1977). The purpose of this test is to ensure there is a similarity on some of the main criteria among the participants and the total population. This test is also to ensure that there is no significant difference between the respondents and the non-respondents, hence indicating that no bias exists.

As proposed by Armstrong and Overton (1977), the data were separated into two periods of time; early response (returns received within one month after distribution), and late response (those returns received after one of distribution). For the purpose to test the non-response-bias, the independent T-test was conducted to compare the responses of the early and late respondents regarding the variables of the study. If the result shows a significant difference between late and early responses, it may indicate the underlying difference between respondent and non-respondent (Armstrong and Overton, 1977). The T-test test was carried out between the 80 early respondents and 43 late respondents. All variables, namely, financial assets, physical assets, technological assets, intellectual property assets, organizational assets, capabilities and port performance. Table 4.1 shows small differences of the mean score between the two groups (early and late response) of each construct, which indicates that the two groups of respondents were almost similar on their perceptions over the undertaken constructs.

Table 4.1: Early and Late Responses Descriptive Statistics Test (n=123)

Variable	**Responses**	**N**	**Mean**	**Std. Deviation**	**Std. Error Mean**
Finance Assets	Early	81	15.235	2.405	.267
	Late	42	16.333	1.996	.308
Physical Assets	Early	81	21.346	2.555	.284
	Late	42	22.929	1.968	.304
Technological Assets	Early	81	15.728	2.275	.253
	Late	42	17.310	1.787	

.276
Organizational
Assets
Early
81
27.901
3.816
.424
Late
42
29.738
3.486
.538
Intellectual Property Assets
Early
81
12.136
1.634
.182
Late
42
12.476
1.671
.258
Capabilities
Early
81
28.914
4.856
.540
Late
42
32.190
3.133
.483
Port Performance
Early
81
14.185
3.009
.334
Late
42
14.571
1.902
.293

However, before concluding the equality of variances of the two groups, Levene's test of the equality of means was examined. The results in Table 4.2 showed that there were no significant differences between late and early respondents across all the variables and from this, it can be concluded that the equality of variances for the two groups was supported at the 0.001 level of significance.

Table 4.2: Independent Sample t-test Results for Non-Response Bias (n=123)

Variable	Construct	Levene's Test for Equality of Variances		t-test for Equality of Means		
		F	Sig.	t	df	Sig. (2-tailed)
Tangible Resources	**Finance Assets**	1.860	.175	-2.541	121	.012
	Physical Assets	2.171	.143	-3.509	121	.001
	Technolo-gicalAssets	.636	.427	-3.918	121	.000
Intangible Resources	**Organiza-tionalAssets**	.465	.497	-2.606	121	.010
	IntellectualProperty Assets	.109	.742	-1.087	121	.279
	Capabilities	4.859	.029			

-3.962
121
.000
Port Perfor-mance
Port Perfor-mance
2.318
.130
-.756
121
.451

4.4Demographic Distribution of the Respondents

The respondents' demographic characteristics are listed in Table 4.3, which shows that number of respondents by port, number of respondent by department, number of respondent by current position and year of service and age, gender and academic qualification.

Table 4.3: Sampling Profile of the Respondents
Demographic Characteristic
Category
Frequency
Percentage
Cumulative Percent %
Number of respondents by Port
PENANG PORT
24
19.5
19.5
KUANTAN PORT CONSORTIUM
19
15.4
35.0
PORT OF TANJUNG PELEPAS
10
8.1
43.1
LUMUT PORT
10
8.1
51.2
JOHOR PORT
17
13.8
65.0
NORTHPORT
23
18.7

83.7
WESTPORT
16
13.0
96.7
LANGKAWI PORT
4
3.3
100.0
Total
123
100.0
Number of Respondent by Department
FINANCE
13
10.6
10.6
HUMAN RESOURCE
27
22.0
32.5
OPERATION
23
18.7
51.2
ENGINEERING
16
13.0
64.2
MARINE
5
4.1
68.3
CORPORATE COMMUNICATION
11
8.9
77.2
IT
14
11.4
88.6
SECURITY
2
1.6
90.2
ADMINISTRATION
6
4.9

95.1
OTHERS
6
4.9
100.0
Total
123
100.0
FINANCE
13
10.6
10.6
Number of Respondent by Current Position
GENERAL MANAGER
9
7.3
7.3
MANAGER
54
43.9
51.2
ASSISTANT MANAGER
18
14.6
65.9
SENIOR EXECUTIVE
32
26.0
91.9
EXECUTIVE
9
7.3
99.2
OTHERS PLEASE STATE
1
.8
100.0
Total
123
100.0
Year of service
0-5
24
19.5
19.5
5-10
37
30.1

49.6
10-20
35
28.5
78.0
> 20 YEARS
27
22.0
100.0
Total
123
100.0
Gender
Male
85
68.5
Female
38
31.5
Age
20-29
12
9.8
30-39
46
37.4
40-49
39
31.7
>50
26
21.1
Academic qualification
SPM/STPM
2
16.3
Certificate/Diploma
34
27.6
Bachelor
61
49.6
Master/PhD
26
21.1

Out of 123 respondents that have completed the survey, Penang Port represents the highest number of respondents with 24 respondents (19.5%) followed by North Port 23 respondents (18.7%), Kuantan 19 respondents Port (15.4%), Johor Port 17 respondents (17%) and West Port 16 respondents (13%). Sabah and Port of Tanjung Pelepas both have 10 respondents (8.1 %) while Bintulu Port has the lowest number of respondents with only 4 (3.3%).

As shown in Table 4.3, the respondents of this study work in various departments with human resource top the list with 27 respondents (22%). Operation department is next with 23 respondents (18.7%) and followed by engineering department 16 (13%), IT department 14 (11.4%), finance department 13 (10.6%) and corporate communication department 11 (8.9%). Both administration and other departments have 6 respondents (4.9%) while marine department consists of 5 respondents (4.1%). Security department meanwhile is represented by 2 respondents only (1.6%).

Table 4.3 shows that 9 (7.3%) of them are general managers while 54 (43.9%) are managers, 19 (14.6%) of the respondents are assistant manager and the remaining respondents which is 42 (34.3%) of them are senior executives.

For the length of working experience or year of services, half of the respondents or 72 (58.6%) of them have been working at the port for more than ten years. This is not surprising because seaport industry needs skilled and semi-skilled labors with vast experience in this field. This is shown in Table 4.3.

The above table also summarizes the age, gender and academic qualification of the respondents. Port services notably are male dominated industry and it shows in this study as majorities (68.5%) of the respondents are male, while only 31.5% are female. Majority of the respondent's age is in between 30 to 49 years old (85 respondents or 69.1%). 26 respondents are more than 50 years old (21.1%) while the other 12 are in between 20 to 29 years of age. For educational background, majority 87 (70.7%) of the respondents hold bachelor degree, master or PhD. It is then followed by certificate or diploma 34 (27.6%) and 2 (16.3%) are SPM holders.

4.5Descriptive Statistics of Variables

Descriptive statistics for the final list of variables of the study are shown in Table 4.4. For ease the interpretation, the ranges of five-point Likert scale were categorized into equal size of low, moderate and high. Therefore, scores less than 2.33{3/4+ lowest value (1)} is considered low; score of 3.67 {highest value (5-4/3)} is considered high and those in between considered moderate. Furthermore, likert scale is one type of rating scale which extensively used in organisational research since it lends itself to more sophisticated data analysis (Sekaran, 2005, p.196).

From Table 4.4, the mean value of tangible resources (financial assets, physical and technological assets) in the range of 3.14 and 3.57. Clearly respondents exhibit medium level of influence of tangible resources namely financial assets, physical and technological assets that contribute towards achieving higher port performance. However, for the intangible resources namely intellectual property assets, organisational assets and capabilities, the mean values of these variables fall in the range of 3.74 and 4.51. Clearly respondents exhibit higher level of influence of intangible resources that improving to higher port performance.

Table 4.4: Descriptive Statistics of the Constructs

Variable

Construct

N

Minimum

Maximum

Mean

Std. Deviation

Tangible Resources

Finance Assets

123
10.00
21.00
15.61
2.32

Physical Assets

123
13.00
25.00
21.89
2.48

Technological
Assets

123
11.00
20.00
16.27
2.24

Intangible Resources
Organizational
Assets

123
19.00
35.00
28.53
3.79

Intellectual Property Assets

123
8.00
15.00
12.25
1.65

Capabilities

123
15.00
35.00
30.03
4.60

Port Performance
Port Performance

123
4.00
18.00
14.32
2.68

4.6 Testing Normality using Skewness and Kurtosis

Two analyses namely skewness and kurtosis were carried out to test the normality of data distribution. The former analysis displayed normality of data with output values between ±3 while the kurtosis analysis also displayed normality with the output values of between ±10 (Kline, 1998). Table 4.5 displays the outcome of the two analyses.

Table 4.5: Testing Normality using Skewness and Kurtosis

Variable	Construct	N	Mean	Skewness		Kurtosis	
		Statistic	Statistic	Statistic	Std. Error	Statistic	Std. Error
Tangible Resources	**Finance Assets**	123	15.6098	.055	.218	-.461	.433
	Physical Assets	123	21.8862	-.654	.218	.367	.433
	Technological Assets	123	16.2683	-.240	.218	-.417	.433
Intangible Resources	**Organizational Assets**	123	28.5285	-.353	.218	-.524	.433

Intellectual Property Assets
123
12.2520
-.245
.218
-.724
.433
Capabilities
123
30.0325
-1.079
.218
.977
.433
Port Performance
Port Performance
123
14.32
-1.667
.218
3.132
.433

4.7Goodness of Measures

Generally, in empirical research, the measurement instruments must have an acceptable level of validity and reliability for two main reasons. Firstly, reliable scales ensure that the measures produce identical results if used repeatedly in different countries, different fields and for longitudinal studies. Secondly, valid scales can increase the confidence that the empirical research findings accurately reflect the proposed construct.

4.7.1 Reliability Analysis

Reliability analysis is very important for empirical research. It raises the confidence that the empirical finding accurately reflect the proposed construct (Moore, 1998). According to Flynn and Sakakibara (1994), the reliability of a scale indicates how free it is from random error. Cronbach's coefficient alpha determines whether the instrument is internally consistent and Nunally (1978) recommended a minimum level .7 for the instrument to be considered reliable. Below is the reliability of each variable for this study.

Cronbach's Alpha can be considered as perfectly adequate indication of the internal consistency, and thus of realibility (Sekaran, 2000). The acceptable value for Cronbach's Alpha is .70, although it may decrease to .50 in exploratory research (Hair et al., 2007). Table 4.8 summarized the reliability test of the measures (after taking into consideration of deleted items). As shown in Table 4.6, the Cronbach Alpha's of the measures were comfortably above minimum acceptable level of .50. For this reason, all measures were reliable and acceptable, and thus providing strong support for all variable components.

Table 4.6: Result of Reliability Analysis

Variable	Construct	Number of Items	Initial Cronbach's Alpha	Items Deleted	Final Cronbach's Alpha
Tangible Resources	Finance Assets	4	.718	Nil	.718
	Physical Assets	5	.881	Nil	.881
	Technological Assets	4	.808	Nil	.808
Intangible Resources	Organizational Assets	3	.778	Nil	.778
	Intellectual Property Assets	7	.896	Nil	.896
	Capabilities	7	.937	Nil	.937
Port Performance	Port Performance	4	.907	Nil	.907

Total items
34

4.7.2 Construct Validity

All scales used in this study were derived from previous studies. First draft of the questionnaire was discussed with a few lecturers before it was pilot tested via face-to-face survey with 34 officers at Penang Port Sdn. Bhd. An earlier questionnaire with 45 item measuring tangible resources, intangible resources and port performance were replaced with the final version that had only 36 items after going through the process discussed in the previous chapter. Therefore, content validity is assumed to be fulfilled in this study.

For the validity test, factor analysis is used to define the underlying structure in data matrix. It is also used to ascertain whether the measurement used in this study has construct validity. In this study, all items measuring the construct of port performance, physical assets, financial assets, IT assets, organisational assets, reputational assets, intellectual property assets and port capabilities. The factor analysis used is based on principal component method with Varimax rotation of all components was adopted for this study.

Factor Analysis of Financial Assets: The below table shows the factors loading financial assets which are between .694 - .769 indicating all items that represent each research variable was 0.5 more, indicating the item met the standard of validity analysis. All research variables exceeded the acceptable standard of Kaiser-Mayer-Olkin's value of 0.6 (Pallant, 2001) which is .705., and Barlett's test of sphericity was highly significant (p=.00). Furthermore, all research variables had eigenvalue greater than 1 and the items for each research variable exceeded factor loading of 0.50 (Hair et al., 2006).

Table 4.7: Result of Factor Analysis for Financial Assets

Variable
Construct
Items
Factor Loading
Variance %
KMO
EigenValue
Tangible Resources
Financial Assets
FIN1
.769
55%
0.705
2.196
FIN2
.744

FIN3
.694

FIN4

.755

Factor Analysis of Physical Assets: Table below the factors loading physical assets which are between .811 - .858 indicating all items that represent each research variable was 0.5 more, indicating the item met the standard of validity analysis. All research variables exceeded the acceptable standard of Kaiser-Mayer-Olkin's value of 0.6 (Pallant, 2001) which is .787., and Barlett's test of sphericity was highly significant (p=.00). Furthermore, all research variables had eigenvalue greater than 1 and the items for each research variable exceeded factor loading of 0.50 (Hair et al., 2006).

Table 4.8: Result of Factor Analysis for Physical Assets

Variable	Construct	Items	Factor Loading	Variance %	KMO	EigenValue
Tangible Resources	Physical Assets	PHY1	.811	68%	0.787	3.403
		PHY2	.813			
		PHY3	.831			
		PHY4	.858			
		PHY5	.811			

Factor Analysis of Technological Assets: Table below table shows the factors loading technological assets which are between .662-882 indicating all items that represent each research variable was 0.5 more, indicating the item met the standard of validity analysis. All research variables exceeded the acceptable standard of Kaiser-Mayer-Olkin's value of 0.6 (Pallant, 2001) which is .791., and Barlett's test of sphericity was highly significant (p=.00). Furthermore, all research variables had eigenvalue greater than 1 and the items for each research variable exceeded factor loading of 0.50 (Hair et al., 2006).

Table 4.9: Result of Factor Analysis for Technological Assets

Variable	Construct	Items

Factor Loading
Variance %
KMO
EigenValue
Tangible Resources
Technological Assets
IT1
.836
66%
0.791
2.652
IT2
.882

IT3
.859

IT4
.662

Factor Analysis of Organizational Assets: Table below table shows the factors loading intellectual property assets which are between .602-.855 indicating all items that represent each research variable was 0.5 more, indicating the item met the standard of validity analysis. All research variables exceeded the acceptable standard of Kaiser-Mayer-Olkin's value of 0.6 (Pallant, 2001) which is .854., and Barlett's test of sphericity was highly significant (p=.00). Furthermore, all research variables had eigenvalue greater than 1 and the items for each research variable exceeded factor loading of 0.50 (Hair et al., 2006).

Table 4.10: Result of Factor Analysis for Organizational Assets

Variable
Construct
Items
Factor Loading
Variance %
KMO
EigenValue
Intangible Resources
Organizational Assets
OA1
.723
62%
0.854
4.338
OA2
.809

OA3
.835

OA4
.835

OA5
.855
OA6
.820
OA7
.602

Factor Analysis of Intellectual Property Assets: Table below shows the factors loading intellectual property assets which are between .671 - .855 indicating all items that represent each research variable was 0.5 more, indicating the item met the standard of validity analysis. All research variables exceeded the acceptable standard of Kaiser-Mayer-Olkin's value of 0.6 (Pallant, 2001) which is .680., and Barlett's test of sphericity was highly significant (p=.00). Furthermore, all research variables had eigenvalue greater than 1 and the items for each research variable exceeded factor loading of 0.50 (Hair et al., 2006).

Table 4.11: Result of Factor Analysis for Intellectual Property Assets

Variable
Construct
Items
Factor Loading
Variance %
KMO
EigenValue
Intangible Resources
Intellectual Property Assets
IPA1
.924
77%
0.680
2.313
IPA2
.888

IPA3
.819

Factor Analysis of Capabilities: Table above table shows the factors loading intellectual property assets which are between .713-.921 indicating all items that represent each research variable was 0.5 more, indicating the item met the standard of validity analysis. All research variables exceeded the acceptable standard of Kaiser-Mayer-Olkin's value of 0.6 (Pallant, 2001) which is .863., and Barlett's test of sphericity was highly significant (p=.00). Furthermore, all research variables had eigenvalue greater than 1 and the items for each research variable exceeded factor loading of

0.50 (Hair et al., 2006).

Table 4.12: Result of Factor Analysis for Capabilities

Variable	Construct	Items	Factor Loading	Variance %	KMO	EigenValue
Intangible Resources	Capabilities	CAP1	.885	73%	0.863	5.109
		CAP2	.857			
		CAP3	.914			
		CAP4	.926			
		CAP5	.861			
		CAP6	.713			
		CAP7	.806			

Factor Analysis of Port Performance: Table below shows the factors loading for port performance which are between .808 and .905 indicating all items that represent each research variable was 0.5 more, indicating the item met the standard of validity analysis. All research variables exceeded the acceptable standard of Kaiser-Mayer-Olkin's value of (Pallant, 2001) which is .799, and Barlett's test of sphericity was highly significant (p=.00). Furthermore, all research variables had eigenvalue greater than 1 and the items for each research variable exceeded factor loading of 0.50 (Hair et al., 2006).

Table 4.13: Result of Factor Analysis for Port Performance

Variable	Construct	Items	Factor Loading	Variance %	KMO	EigenValue

Port Performance
Port Performance
PP1
.918
79%
0.800
3.156
PP2
.839

PP3
.951

PP4
.840

Factor Analysis of the Whole Variables: As mentioned earlier, variables in the questionnaires grouped into 3 main categories. The first categories is the port performance (4 items) second is the tangible resources (15 items) and third components is the intangible resources (17 items). Based from the result of the Principal component method, the result suggested that all variables should be grouped into seven main categories. According to Hair et al., (2006), the final determination of the number of factors must wait until the results are rotated and the factor are interoperated. They recommended that the researcher next employs a rotational method to achieve simpler and theoretically more meaningful factor solution. Because many components were extracted, it is important to look at the scree plot (Figure 2). We need to look for change (or elbow) in the shape of the plot, because only component above this point are retained. In this study, it is quite a clear break between the sixth and seventh components.

The result of factor analysis of 36 questions provided seven factors with relative explanatory power (Eigenvalues) of 13.182, 3.089, 2.583, 1.769, 1.576, 1.392 and 1.126 respectively, and it is clear that their Eigenvalues exceed one. These seven factors captured a total value of variance of 72.69 percent of the total variance of the items. Furthermore, the loading greater than .50 which is a minimum level required for a sample of size 120 and above (Hair et al., 2006). Table 5.14 below displays the result of factor analysis of all the variables. It omitted the items that violated the criterion set by Hair et al. (1998). Items were deleted when they showed either low factor (<.50) or high cross loading (>.35). As a result, the remaining items ranged from .602-.951, which were acceptable based on the criterion set.

Figure 2: Scree Plot of Factor Analysis

The overall value Kaiser-Meyer-Olkin was found to be .876. A close inspection of individual MSA value shows that all 34 items have values within the acceptable range that between .602-.951. However, 2 items that score below .50 were deleted. Furthermore, the results of the Barlett's test was highly significant (p=.00). This indicates that the assumptions of factor analysis were met.

On the basis of factor loading, the 7 factors remained are named accordingly. The grouping of items suggested by factor analysis is similar to the proposed categories of tangible and intangible assets. Item related to financial assets remain four items (TR 1 – TR 4). The second factor which is physical assets (TR 5 – TR 9) contains 5 items remain in the same group. The third factor was labelled as technological assets contain 6 items. However, two items from this group were deleted as the factor loading is less than .50.

The fourth factor which is Intellectual Property Assets (IR 1 - IR 3) which has three items also remain in the same group. The fifth factor contains 4 items (IR 4 - IR 7) which is organizational assets also remain in the same group. The sixth factor which is reputational assets which has 3 items (IR 8 - IR 10) was merged with the organizational assets. The sixth and the seventh factor which is capabilities and port performance has 6 items (TR 11- TR 17) and four items (PP 1 – PP 4) respectively also remain in the same group remain in the same group as the factor loading greater is than 0.5.

In general, result of the exploratory analysis on the main variables proposed in the conceptual framework indicates dimensions that are similar to the original dimensions. Variables such as financial assets, physical assets, intellectual property assets capabilities and port performance remained as one separate dimension. On the other hand variables of organizational assets and reputational assets are combined into one group. Table 5.14 shows the comparison between the original dimensions and the final dimensions.

Table 4.14: Total number of items before and after factor analysis

ORIGINAL DIMENSION

TOTAL ITEMS

BEFORE FACTOR ANALYSIS

TOTAL ITEMS AFTER FACTOR ANALYSIS

INDEPEN-DENT

VARIABLES

Tangible Resources

Financial Assets

4

4

Physical Assets
5
5
Technological Assets
6
4
Intangible
Resources
Intellectual Property Assets
3
3
Organisational Assets
4
3(merge)
7
Reputational Assets
Capabilities
7
7
DEPENDENT
VARIABLES
Port Performance
4
4
TOTAL ITEMS
36
34

4.8Pearson Correlation Analysis

According to Hair et al. (2010), discriminant validity is the degree to which conceptually similar concept is distinct and the empirical test is the correlation measures. The correlation should be low, demonstrating discriminant validity is established. The second method is to examine the discriminant analysis; the correlations between factors should not exceed 0.7. A correlation greater than 0.7 indicates a majority of shared variance (0.7 * 0.7 = 49% shared variance).

In order to access discriminant validity, correlation analysis is used to evaluate the measures, a comparison was made between the loading of an item with its associated factor (construct) to its cross loading. The Pearson correlation coefficient was performed to obtain an understanding the relationship between all the variables study. The Pearson correlation coefficient r can only take values from -1 and + 1 which indicate a perfect negative or positive correlation among variables (Coakes & Steed, 2007). However, different authors suggest different interpretations of the r between 0 and 1. Cohen (1988) suggests the following guidelines:

r = 0.10 to .29 or = -0.1 to - 0.29 Small
r = 0.30 to 0.49 or = -0.30 to - 0.49 Medium
r = 0.50 to 1.0 or = -0.50 to - 1.0 Large

Table 4.15 shows that overall correlation value is below .50 which indicates a weak association between variables. The largest and significant correlation coefficient value is between port capabilities and intellectual property assets of .608. In addition, three variables (physical assets, organizational assets and capabilities) are significantly correlated to port performance at medium *r* scores between .255 and .444. However, other variables (financial assets, technological assets and intellectual property assets) score weak correlation coefficient value which fall between .131 and .142. Based on the results of the correlation analysis, the values of all variables are less than .9. This indicates that there is no multicollinearity exist between variables.

Table 4.15: Results of Pearson Correlation Analysis

Variable Construct	1	2	3	4	5	6	7
Tangible Resources							
1) Finance Assets	1						
2) Physical Assets	.490**	1					
3) Technological Assets	.360**	.555**	1				
Intangible Resources							
4) Organizational Assets	.228*	.279**	.357**	1			
5) Intellectual Property Assets	.178*	.238**	.303**	.791**	1		
6) Capabilities	.259**	.416**	.428**	.575**	.608**	1	
Port Performance							
7) Port Performance	.131						

.147
.142
.255**
.314**
.444**
1

Correlation is significant at the 0.05 level (1-tailed). ** Correlation is significant at the 0.01 level (1-tailed).

PP=Port Performance FIN = Financial Assets, PHY = Physical Assets, IT = Technological Assets, IPA = Intellectual Property Assets, OA = Organisational Assets, CAP = Capabilities.

4.9Multiple Linear Regression Analysis

In order to answer the research questions that address the relationship and the influence of tangible and intangible resources on port performance the regression analyses were conducted. However, before conducting the analysis, the data were first examined to detect whether there is any serious violations from the basic assumption underlying the regression analysis, namely linearity, normality and homoscedasticity (Hair et. al, 1998).

4.9.1 Diagnostic Tests

In order to ensure data quality, before multiple regression analysis was conducted, major assumptions that relate to multiple regression analysis were confirmed. These assumptions have to be met in order to guarantee that the model's prediction of actual errors originate from the absence of variables' associations as opposed to the data characteristics that fall short of accommodating the regression method (Hair et al., 2010). These assumptions are multicollinearity, normality, linearity and homoscesdasticity (Hair et al., 2010) and the discussion of these assumptions are described in detail in the next subsections.

Checking the Multicollinearity: Multicollinearity refers to high correlations among independent variables, whereas singularity occurs when perfect correlations exist among independent variables. The multicollinearity is examined by looking at variance influenced factor (VIF), which indicates of the effect the other independent variables have on the standard error of regression coefficient. VIF has direct relation to tolerance value. Hair et. al, (2006) agreed that VIF should be close 1.00 to indicate little or multicollinearity.

Overall, the inspection on data revealed that there was no serious violation of the basic assumptions. Therefore, the use of regression for subsequent analysis is appropriate. The interpretation of the regression analysis is based on standardized coefficient beta (ß) and R^2, which provides evidence whether to support or not to support the hypotheses stated earlier in the chapter.

Multicollinearity refers to the level of the variable's impact that can be explained by other variables (Hair et al., 2010). In other words, increase in multicollinearity leads to the increase in the difficulty of interpretation of different variables' affects. In this study, the researcher made use of the tolerance value and Variance Inflation Factor (VIF) to examine the occurrence of multicollinearity among variables. Specifically, tolerance is the variable's variability that cannot be explained by other variables (Hair et al., 2010) whereas the VIF indicator refers to the tolerance variable's reciprocal element.

Table below displays the tolerance values of the study variables and they range is 0.958 while the VIF values range is 1.044. The tolerance values are higher than 0.1 and the VIF are all below 10 as suggested by Hair et al. (2010) indicating that both value sets are within the recommended range and thus it can be concluded that multicollinearity issue does not exist.

Table 4.16: Multicollinearity Test

Variable	Construct	Tolerance Value	VIF
Tangible Resources	Finance Assets	.744	1.345
	Physical Assets	.567	1.763
	Technological Assets	.626	1.597
Intangible Resources	Organizational Assets	.350	2.857
	Intellectual Property Assets	.336	2.976
	Capabilities	.527	1.899

a. Dependent Variable: Port Performance

Testing the Normality of the Error Terms

Linearity is described as the residuals reflecting a straight line relationship with the dependent variables predicted scores (Pallant, 2001). In this study, linearity was examined through scatterplots. Specifically, the histogram and the normality probability plot (p-p plots) were employed along with the kolmogorov-smirnov skewness and kurtosis values to confirm normality. The results are presented in Figures 3 and 4 indicating that data distribution stayed within the normal curve – in other words, data displayed normal distribution.

Figure 3: Histogram of the Regression Residuals

Figure 4: Normal Probability Plot

The normality assumption was also confirmed via examining P-P plot and Q-Q plot of both dependent variables. According to the plots, data formed a straight line in graphs revealing normal distribution of data.

Linearity Test

A linear relationship is considered in multiple regression analysis between the dependent and predictor variables, where linearity is established through the residual plots. Nevertheless, these plots are not considered as empirical method and thus scholars have proposed several other methods. Figure 5 below shows a random scatter plot that confirms linearity assumption based on Hair et al.'s (2010) recommendations.

Figure 5: Scatterplot of the Residuals

Homoscedasticity

As suggested by Hair et al. (2006), the existence of homoscedasticity can be examined by plotting the residual (studentized) against the predicted dependent values and comparing them to the null plot. The scatter plot in Figure 5 shows no discernible patterns, thus indicating homoscedasticity in the multivariate (the set of independent variables) case.

4.10 Testing of Hypotheses

5.10.1 Multiple Regression Analysis of the Financial Asset, Physical Assets, Technological Assets, Organizational Assets, Intellectual Property Assets and Capabilities on Port Performance

Table 4.17: Regression Results of Model

(Dependent= Port Performance)

Variables	**Standardized Coefficients**	**t-value**	**Sig.**
	Beta		
Finance Assets	.050	.526	.600
Physical Assets	-.039	-.357	.722
Technological Assets	-.051	-.492	.624
Organizational Assets	-.078	-.559	.577
Intellectual Property Assets	.125	.878	.382
Capabilities	.438	3.846	.000
R^2	0. 207		
Adjusted R^2	0.166		
F-value	5.061		
F-Significant			

0.000

Table 4.18: Results from the Multiple Regression Analysis

Variables	**Beta**	**T-value**	**Significant**
Financial Assets	.050	.526	.600
Physical Assets	-.039	-.357	.722
Technological Assets	.050	-.492	.624
Intellectual Property Assets	-.051	-.559	.577
Organisational Assets	-.078	.878	.382
Capabilities	.125	3.846	.000
R^2	.207		
R Square Adjusted	.166		
F	5.061		
Significant	.000		

a. **Relationship of Tangible Resources and Port Performance**

The first research question for this research is "Do physical assets, financial assets and technological assets have significant relationships with port performance?". In this analysis, financial assets, physical assets and technological assets are treated as the independent variable, whereas port performance as the dependent variable. The outcome from the multiple regression analysis shows in Table 4.18. Based from the result, the significance level of all variables are more than .05 which indicates that all tangible resources does not have a significant contribution to the prediction of port performance.

Based on the results, displayed three important findings:

H1: Financial assets was not significantly related to port performance, therefore the hypothesis 1 was rejected.

H2: Physical assets was not significantly related to port performance, therefore the hypothesis 2 was rejected.

H3: Technological assets was not significantly related to port performance, therefore the hypothesis 3 was rejected.

In sum, this results show that financial assets, physical assets and technological assets do not add as important determinants of port performance.

a. **Relationship of Intangible Resources and Port Performance**

The second research question for this research is "Do physical assets, financial assets and technological assets have significant relationships with port performance?". In this analysis, intellectual property assets, organizational assets and capabilities are treated as the independent variable, whereas port performance as the dependent variable. Based from the result, the significance level of intellectual property assets and organizational assets are more than .05 which indicates that these variables does not have a significant contribution to the prediction of port performance. However, for capabilities, the result shows that relationship between port capabilities and port performance is significant (F=16.044, sig=0.00). The value of R^2 is .20.7, which means that 20.7 percent of the variance in portperformance is explained significantly by port capabilities. Absolute beta values are used to compare contribution of each independent variable to the dependent variable. The beta coefficient for this variable is .125 and T-value is 3.846. This indicates that port capabilities have made unique and statistically contribution to the prediction of port performance. Based on the results, displayed three important findings:

H4: Intellectual Property assets were not significantly related to port performance, therefore the hypothesis 3 was rejected.

H5: Organizational assets was not significantly related to port performance, therefore the hypothesis 3 was rejected.

H6: Capabilities was positively and significantly related to port performance, therefore the hypothesis 6 was accepted.

In sum, this results show that intellectual property assets, organizational assets do not add as important determinants of port performance, whereas port capabilities do add as important determinants of port performance.

c. **Multiple regressions for Factors Influencing Port Performance-Comparison between Tangible and Intangible Resources**

The final research question is "Do port intangible resources have more influence on port performance than port tangible resources?". Based on the result from the multiple regression analysis above, it shows that port intangible resources specifically port capabilities give more achieving higher port performance as compare to port tangible resources (financial assets, physical assets and technological assets). Based on the results, displayed the last finding:

H7: Port intangible resources have more influence in achieving higher port performance than port tangible resources. Therefore, the hypothesis 7 was accepted.

4.11Summary of the Chapter

This chapter discussed the empirical results of this study. The test of non-response bias revealed no statistically significant between early and late response. Therefore, the issue of non-response bias did not significantly affect the generalizability of the findings in this study.

The descriptive statistics showed that, in general, the result shows that port infrastructures scores high level in influencing port performance among tangible assets, whereas port organizational policies scores high level of in port performance among intangible port resources. Further, the standard deviation demonstrate that the variation of all port resources among respondents were moderate.

To examine the relationship between port resources and port performance as well as the factors influencing port performance, regression analyses were conducted. The tests of the hypotheses revealed that four of the hypotheses created for this study were rejected (hypotheses 1, 2 3 and 4) and two pf hypotheses the hypotheses were accepted (hypothesis 4 and 6).

CHAPTER FIVE: DISCUSSION OF PORT PERFORMANCE

CHAPTER FIVE: DISCUSSION OF PORT PERFORMANCE

5.1 Introduction

This chapter attempts to discuss the findings of the data analysis stage as described in the previous chapter. The discussions are organized based on the hypotheses of the study. It is then followed by discussions on the limitation of the study, and its contribution to both the theoretical and organizational aspects. This last chapter then concludes with the conclusion and direction for future research.

5.2 Discussion of Findings

The main objective of this study is to examine the influence of port tangible and intangible resources on port performance based on the framework of Resource-Based View. Revisiting the study objective, this study was undertaken to seek answers to several research questions. (1) Do physical assets, financial assets and technological assets have significant relationships with port performance? (2) Do intellectual property assets, organizational assets and capabilities have significant relationships with port performance? and (3) Do port intangible resources have more influence on port performance than port tangible resources ?

As noted in Chapter 4, exploratory principal component factor analyses were utilized to test the factorial validity of the measures in this study. The analyses undertaken produced various dimensions of the various dimensions of the port resources and capabilities which included port resources and intangible resources with port performance. The hypotheses were then reformulated using these new dimensions. The internal consistency of the measures was then tested by computing the reliability coefficient. Finally the data were analyzed using regression analyses to test the hypotheses of the study. The .05 level of significant was used as the critical level of decision making regarding the hypotheses.

Table 5.1: Summary of Results

HYPHOTHESIS

FINDINGS

H1 :There is a significant relationship between financial assets and port performance.

Rejected

H2 :There is a significant relationship between physical assets and port performance.

Rejected

H3 :There is a significant relationship between technological assets port performance

Rejected

H4 :There is a significant relationship between intellectual property and performance.

Rejected

H5 : There is a significant relationship between organization assets and port performance.

Rejected

H6 :There is a significant relationship between capabilities and port performance.

Accepted

H7 : Port intangible resources have more influence achieving higher port performance than port tangible resources.

Accepted

Table 5.1 shows the results of the hypothesis testing. It details each proposed relationship whether it is accepted or not.

For the purpose of testing the research hypotheses, port resources are divided into six resources constructs namely: physical assets, financial asset, port technological assets, intellectual property assets, organizational assets, and capabilities. With these constructs, seven series of hypotheses are created to find out which of the port resources and capabilities are more important to port performance. These hypotheses however assert that port resources that are intangible in nature have more influence to port performance than tangible resource.

In order to answer the first research question, this study constructed three hypotheses. The following section discusses each hypothesis in detail.

Hypothesis 1:

H1: There is a significant relationship between financial assets and port performance. (rejected)

The first hypothesis assesses the relationship between port financial assets and port performance. As suggested by the RBV theoretical perspective, tangible assets only contribute little or nothing to a firm's competitive advantage. Indeed, Amit and Shoemaker (1993) and Michalisin, Smith, and Kline (1997) for example, suggest that the resources that drive a firm's success are intangible, rather than tangible, in nature. Similarly, Soo (2001) suggests that because tangible resources are not valuable, rare, inimitable, or non-substitutable, they are rendered non-strategic to a firm's success. With regard to firm's financial resources, it is one of the tangible assets and thus is not a source of competitive advantage (Amit & Schoemaker, 1993). This is because financial resources are easily observed and imitated by competitors (Barney, 1991). Hence, the hypothesis proposes that financial assets have no relationship with port performance.

The result from the correlation analysis of this study shows that financial assets are not significantly associated with port performance. It shows that financial assets do not have an additional explanatory power in predicting port performance. This result confirms the previous results in RBV literature which show that firm financial assets are not important sources of firm competitive advantage. There are a few possible answers why port financial assets do not contribute to port performance in the context of the port industry.

Financial assets in this study include cash in hand and in the bank earned from port operations, raised financial capital, for example from secured bank loans or equity from the issuance of shares or bonds, financial investment and port investment for the purpose of building physical assets that are used in the provision of port services (such as port seaway access dredging of its harbour), its highway access such as pavement and traffic lights and its rail access such as building of rail tracks. Hence, one of the reasons why port financial assets do not have an additional explanatory power of predicting port performance is that, these assets are tangible and easily can be imitated by potential competitors (Amit Sheoemaker, 1993; Teece, 1998a; Barney, 2001b).Itami and Roehl (1987) and Wernerfelt (1989) argued that financial and physical assets have relatively fixed long-run capacity whereas intangible resources have relatively unlimited capacity.

Due to the higher cost of port investment and port operation, ports need to have larger financial investments in order to be equipped with port infrastructures and superstructures, for example sophisticated equipment, cranes, or in dredging channels to meet the market demand for a large number of ships and to stay competitive in the market (Cullinane, Ping, & Teng-Fei, 2005). Without port investment in port infrastructure and facilities, ports will not be able to produce efficient service in handling the volume of cargoes. However, financial credibility alone does not create the element of competitive advantage.

Previous research on port competitiveness shows that factors that do affect the level of port competitiveness is the level of port efficiency (Tongzon and Heng, 2005). Financial assets and credibility of a port, however, are needed in order to upgrade the level of service and efficiency, thus port financial assets are needed to buy new equipment and infrastructure and provide excellent hinterland services. Financial assets also are needed to improve the level of efficiency by improving the depth of navigational channels and landside accessibility. All these factors require huge financial credibility; thus it indirectly tells that financial assets do have an indirect relationship with port competitiveness and performance. However financial assets only are not enough to ensure ports are able to meet the market demand and stay competitive in the market. Notteboom and Winkelman (2001) stated that investments on infrastructure may not be enough to increase the port performance as shippers are constantly looking at alternative routes in order to reduce total logistics cost.

Hypothesis 2:

H2: There is a significant relationship between physical assets and port performance. (rejected)

The result of the multiple regressions conducted for this study shows that port physical assets do not have a significant influence on port performance. Therefore, port physical assets are not considered as one of the important factors to achieve higher port performance. This finding is consistent with the RBV theory which shows that a firm's physical assets are not an important factor to increase port performance. Based on the RBV theory, physical assets are not considered as a source of competitive advantage, thus they do not have influence on firm performance. In the context of the port industry, port physical assets include the port's geographical location, infrastructure, superstructure, facilities and all the assets that are tangible in nature. These assets are assumed not to have the characteristics of value, rareness, inimitable and non-substitutable (VRIN) and could be easily be imitated by competitors.

Most capital resources at ports, such as container cranes, terminals and port equipment can be readily obtained by competitors with sufficient resources. Therefore, it is unlikely that a port can obtain a sustainable competitive advantage based on capital equipment. Furthermore, many resources possessed by ports can be obtained easily, and therefore cannot be considered to be especially rare or difficult to imitate. Brian Slack (1985) states that port infrastructures do not appear to play an important role in selecting a port of call because it was influenced by price and service considerations offered within the supply chain network.

Tengku (1995) in his PhD thesis highlighted that the important factors contributing to Malaysian port competitiveness are port tariffs, safe handling of cargoes, confidence in port schedules and port service. These factors are more related to capabilities of the port in handling port operation and offering excellent services. However, it cannot be denied that port physical assets are also important in ensuring that port operations are carried out efficiently and effectively. It is only when there is no capabilities role such as employee's skill and expertise that the role of physical assets is not effective in improving port performance.

Yeo et al., (2011) who found that the two important attributes of port competitiveness in Northeast Asia are the hinterland condition and the availability of a berth. Hinterland condition includes professionals and skilled labour in port operations. They explained that the second factor constitute the element of physical assets. However, this is crucial because of the relations between the first and the second factors.

This is because, although the port can provide the best physical assets, without the second factor that is professional and skilled labour, port efficiency, competitiveness and improvement of port performance cannot be achieved. This means, the role of physical assets will become important if it is combined with port capabilities and existing competencies.

Furthermore, Tongzon (2006) argued that one of the critical success factors of PSA is port infrastructure which can handle large numbers of vessels and container flows. However, this factor is important only if it is supported with soft infrastructure in terms of skilled port management and the provision of a wide range of port-related and ship-related services are very effective.

Hypothesis 3:

H3: There is a significant relationship between technological assets and port performance. (rejected)

The result of the correlation analysis shows that port technological assets do not have a positive relationship with port performance. As a result, port technological assets are not considered as important factors that influence port performance. This result confirms the previous RBV studies on firm competitiveness. According to the RBV theory, firm technological assets are one of the assets that have tangible characteristics in nature. Thus they are not considered as a source of competitive advantage. This is because port technological assets have a tendency to be duplicated by the competitors in the long run which will not allow the port to attain an advantage. Even if a competitor fails to duplicate the technology or develop new ones, there still may be 'revolutions' in an industry so that resources that once sustained an advantage for a firm will be no longer valuable (Gordon, Lee, & Lucas, 2005).

There are few a main arguments to answer why port technology is not an important source of port performance. Without human skills and capabilities the port would not be able to utilize the capacity of its technology. Since port efficiency and productivity are crucially important for port performance, the advancement of port technological assets and innovations have made a big impact on port performance. However, again without the managers and employees' skills, ports will not be able to achieve the desired goals and increase port performance.

According to Notteboom and Winkelmans (2001), one of the port differentiation strategies for port operator is providing specific port services in market niches and this can be achieved by offering greater value to the port users based from port specific competencies such as advanced information systems that are inimitable and durable and thus, it is easier to achieve competitive advantages over other competitors. Tongzon (2004) stated that, the introduction of port technology especially information technology will reduce turnaround time for processing information about ship arrivals and departure, loadings and unloading and help to collect individual data on ports or logistics and integrate them to share with customers. Among the advanced technologies used by Malaysian ports are Container Terminal Management System, Synchronous Planning and Real-time Control System, Smart Rail System, Container Freight Station System, Commercial Management Information System and Container Terminal Operating System. However, the competitiveness of a port having advanced technology can only be achieved if the port has some groups of talented and experienced workers to achieve the port's mission and vision. Thus, it will be able to improve port performance and competitiveness. The available technology can only be used if there are employees who are experts in managing the assets. Improvement in port performance cannot be achieved without skills and expertise in port technology.

Hypothesis 4:

H4: There is a significant relationship between intellectual property assets and port performance. (rejected)

Based on the correlation analysis result, port intellectual property assets do not have a significant association with port performance. Hence, this finding does not support the RBV theoretical perspective. In contrast, RBV argued that intellectual property assets have some characteristics of VRIN and this asset is considered as one of the important sources of firm performance. Intellectual property assets such as patents, copyrights, proprietary (or held-in secret) technology, trademark and registered design have long been argued to be important determinants for the overall success of a firm. According to the RBV theory, IPA exhibits the characteristics of resource value, rareness, inimitability and non-substitutability (VRIN) than other tangible assets and therefore, it helps move the firm ahead of their competitors.

In the context of Malaysian the port industry, the result shows that intellectual property assets do not have a significant influence on port performance. According to Lee, Teo and Lim (2000), port operations are conducted using high technology. The source of competitive advantage is based on patented technology will enhance the efficiency of port operation. According to Porter (2003), the Intellectual Property Protection (IPP) in Malaysia is far behind other countries in Asia. Malaysia is ranked 33 compared to other countries. In terms of the efficacy of corporate brand, Malaysian is ranked 44. This shows that Malaysian's firms still do not emphasize the importance of intellectual property assets in improving the firm's performance including port management. In the context of port, the importance of intellectual property assets is less compared to other industries.

Fagerberg, Srholec, and Knell (2007) conducted an empirical analysis, based on a sample of 90 countries on different levels of development during 1980–2002, which showed the relevance of technology, capacity and demand competitiveness for growth and development. As Malaysian ports handle more trade and host users whose needs have become more complex, their reliance on technology and the need to have in place adequate capacity, and high level of productivity and efficiency have also increased. Without these, their business cannot grow. Although the advantage of technology should be patented so that it becomes a competitive advantage of a firm that cannot be imitated by the rivals.

The awareness of the importance of intellectual property assets is still negligible in Malaysia as compared to Singapore, where the practice of developing the system and technology among the IT experts is much encouraged. According to Gordon et. al (2005), among the technology that is developed by experts such as PORTNET, CITOS and CIMOS. This technology has contributed to the success and competitive advantage of the Port Singapore Authority (PSA). The inimitable characteristics of these systems are developed by a group of IT experts from the PSA which comprises of dedicated and skilled workers. The technological know-how of the IT group is obtained through experience (since most systems are developed in-house) and by doing this, PSA ensures that the port IT system is not easily tradable and imitated by other competitors.

Hypothesis 5:

H5: There is a significant relationship between organisational assets and port performance.(rejected)

The result of the multiple regression analysis shows that organizational assets do not have a significant influence on port performance. Organizational assets include port's culture, port human resource policies, port contractual agreement, port organizational structure and port reputation. Based on the theoretical perspective, organizational assets are theorized to possess the characteristics of value, rareness, inimitable and non-substitutability (VRIN) with high barriers towards duplication. As a result, they helps to improve port competitiveness and performance.

This finding contradicts with the findings of previous studies (Huselid, 1995; Itami, 1987; Lazear, 2000; Song & Yeo, 2004; Yap & Lam, 2006a) and the RBV theory which stresses on the importance of organizational assets towards firm success. Among the important elements of port organizational asset is the port contractual agreement in the form of vertical and horizontal integration with port maritime players. Notteboom and Rodrigue (2012) argued that by having strategic partnership in the form of vertical or horizontal integration, the port would be able to achieve greater cost-saving and achieve economies of scale by implementing common systems across the terminal network.

According to Ghani and Mahyudin (2014) there a few challenges in managing international strategic alliance in Malaysia. He added that some managers facing difficulties in monitoring operations with in which they may have little familiarity (i.e. markets, distribution systems and legal systems). On top of that, they must also cope with significant geographical separations and bridge cultural boundaries. Consistent with the difficulty of managing international strategic alliances, many of them encounter performance problems and approximately 60 per cent fail or are disbanded resulting from poor monitoring and control practices (Bengi & Sibel, 2011).

In Malaysia, strategic partnership is a form of capacity sharing in order to reach a greater number of destinations without utilizing more vessels. Malaysian companies are member of alliances like the New Grand Alliance comprising MISC, Nippon Yusen Kaisha Line, Orient Overseas Container Line (OOCL), Hapag Lloyd and P& O Nedlloyd (PONL). Important alliances in the East-West trade are the New World Alliance, MAERSK/SeaLand, Tricon, Sino-Japanese Alliance. Similar less powerful groups are the Safari comprising MISC, Mitsui Osk Lines (MOL), PONL, KLine, and Safmarine, the Far East Australia. Nevertheless, more studies need to be conducted to prove that strategic alliance could increase the performance of Malaysian ports.

According to Tongzon (2007), further cooperation and win–win alliances among the major seaports in the Asean region should be explored to make the region more competitive and attractive for foreign manufacturing and logistics firms. For example, in the area of seaport, regional alliances in the form of marketing, cargo handling, training and research which lower overhead and operational costs would be desirable and feasible and would make the region more attractive as distribution centres for logistics companies. However, alliances in terms of price- fixing and profit-sharing would be difficult, if not impossible, especially when these ports are government-owned due to nationalistic and political factors, apart from the tendency for countries to capture the largest slice of the logistics market.

In the context of firm culture, previous studies in Malaysia among public-listed companies shows that firm culture is one of the main factors that encourage employees in attaining their full commitment for organisational success

(Zain, Ishak, & Ghani, 2009). However, in the context of Malaysian ports, this research shows that there is no significant influence of port culture in achieving higher port performance. It is suggested that future research on port competitiveness should explore the effect of port culture toward enhancing port performance. This can provide a clearer picture about the importance of port culture because the port industries might possess a unique culture compared to other industries.

Another element of organizational assets is port reputation. According to Tongzon (2009), one of the important elements of port reputation is the perception of cargo safety and it is more powerful and important than the actual safety. Thus, marketing and promotional efforts by port authorities and operators to highlight the port's positive characteristics and accomplishments could improve the port's reputation. A record of accomplishments and achievements gives assurance to customers in terms of quality and reliability. The latter is eminent for influencing port users' choice of port as it is often the relative perception of customers that supersedes the actual port performance. However, the result of this study shows that there no significant relationship between this factor and higher port performance.

Hypothesis 6:

H6: There is a significant relationship between capabilities assets and port performance. (accepted)

The sixth hypothesis examines the relationship between port capabilities and port performance. Capability is an intangible resource and strategic management scholars argued that it is more important from a strategic point of view, since it brings together more frequently the requirements necessary for producing sustainable advantage to be valuable, rare and difficult to imitate and replace by competitors (Barney, 1991; Grant, 2002).

Capability refers to a firm's capacity to deploy and coordinate different resources, usually in combination, using organizational processes, to affect a desired end (Amit & Schoemaker, 1993; Grant, 1996; Prahalad & Hamel, 1990). Capability has two main features that distinguish it from a resource. First, capability is firm specific since it is embedded in the organization and its processes, while an ordinary resource is not (Makadok, 2001). Secondly, the purpose of capability is to enhance the effectiveness and productivity of resources that a firm possesses in order to accomplish its targets, acting as 'intermediate goods' (Amit & Schoemaker, 1993).

In this study, port capabilities encompassed skills, creativity, know-how, routines and relationship of employees and managers with port external constituents. Based on the result of the correlation analysis, port capabilities do have a positive and significant association with port performance. This association between capabilities and port profitability and performance was expected as this association is central in RBV (Peteraf, 1993) theory. This result also confirms previous research which posit that capabilities contribute positively towards firm performance (Fahy, 2002).

In the context of the port industry, port capabilities are among the important factors in achieving higher port performance. Notteboom and Winkelmans (2001) stated that the best class of port performance and competitiveness can be obtained through enhancing port-core competencies and capabilities that are inimitable and durable. Port capabilities which are based on a complexity of technologies and human skills and know-how will be difficult for competing ports to imitate and it will, therefore, have a higher probability to achieve high performance and gain competitive advantage. However, sustainability of a port's competitive advantage depends on the rate at which the underlying resources and capabilities depreciate in time.

Another recent study which supports this finding is from Notteboom and Rodrigue (2012) which indicate that higher port performance and competitiveness can be achieved when the port possesses capabilities such as in the area of firm size and the realization of economies of scale and scope, market power and marketing skills and technological expertise as well as managerial know-how.

Tongzon (2007) shows that one of the main determinants that influence port performance in the Asean Region is reliability which means that ports should be able to meet the predictable performance e.g. shipping lines' schedules. This needs the skills and competencies of the employees. If a port authority or port operator always incurs delays during operations due to strikes, equipment breakdown, weather, etc, shipping companies and shippers will suffer substantial losses due to such unreliability. Definitely, carriers and shippers will most likely bypass this port even if it offers the most attractive price among its competitors.

Hypothesis 7:

H7: Port intangible resources have more influence in achieving higher port performance than port tangible resources. (accepted)

The last hypothesis was constructed to answer the last question of this study which is "Do the port intangible resources have more influence on port performance than port tangible resources" ?.The final hypothesis offers the most fine-grained level of analysis in the research. Port intangible resources, which include port intellectual property assets, port intellectual property assets, organizational assets and port capabilities, are hypothesized to have a greater influence on port performance as compared to port tangible resources which consist of port physical assets, port financial assets and port technological assets. This hypothesis is indeed supported as the result of the Multiple Regression analysis shows that the intangible resources which are port capabilities have the strongest influence on port performance. However, other intangible assets such as organisational assets and intellectual property assets do not have a significant influence on port performance. The association between intangible resources and performance and competitiveness is not surprising as it is central in the RBV theory (Peteraf, 1993). The findings even confirmed previous studies by Galbreath and Galvin (2004) and (Fahy, 2002) who stated that intangible assets are generally found to be more important determinants of firm success and performance than tangible assets.

Furthermore, the finding of this research shows that among the intangible assets port capabilities have the greatest influence in achieving higher port performance. This finding confirm with the previous RBV-based studies which postulate that capabilities are the most important determinant of firm success (Fahy, 2002; Welbourne & Wright, 1997).

5.3 Theoretical Implication

There are three important theoretical implications that can be derived from this study: (1) conceptual measurement; (2) RBV as a framework for management research; (3) the importance of port capabilities.

5.3.1 Conceptual measurement of the RBV

The uniqueness of the RBV theory as compared to other theories is based from the principle that firms compete on the basis of resource endowment rather than the structural characteristics of industries. The RBV theory posits that firm performance and competitiveness are fundamentally driven by a combination of intangible resources and not by resources that are tangible in nature. To verify such a theory, the researcher had to develop a conceptualization of resources from which to operationalize resource constructs. Given this requirement, the first important theoretical implication arising from this research was with respect to the operationalization and measurement of RBV.

Based from previous RBV studies, most of the researches tended to focus on a very limited resource variable, namely individual intangible resource. However, some researchers agreed that firms do not compete on the basis of a single, intangible resource only, but rather they compete with a system of resources (Foss, 1998; Wernerfelt, 1984). Thus, the first theoretical implication of this study is that it provides comprehensive measurements of a much broader resource base, rather than a specific intangible resources or single proxy measures. Given that firms are a system of tangible and intangible resources (Barney, 1991; Foss, 1998; Wernerfelt, 1984), then testing the empirical assertion of the RBV, in the context of the broader resources pool, is a logical and important step for the validation of the theory (Foss, 1998; Makhija, 2003; Mauri & Michaels, 1998).

This study used a much more precise operationalization of both the intangible and tangible assets with multiple constructs, rather than general proxy measures (such as advertising or research and development expenditure, port productivity and efficiency) which were usually used by previous studies. Resources are the building blocks of a firm's success in the market. So verifying which one is important for success and performance requires precise measurement across multiple construct including both tangible and intangible resources.

5.3.2 RBV as a framework for port management research

The findings from this study suggest a few key points with respect to the RBV and its usefulness to management research. First, the findings clearly shows that there can be an exception to what RBV assume in different industry, financial assets, physical assets and technological assets are not an important determinant of success according to RBV but in the context of port industry, this study proves capabilities is among the most important elements for port performance.

By adopting the RBV theory, this research has succeeded in developing and testing a new conceptual model in analyzing port performance. This study proves the relationship between port capabilities which consist of skills and know-how of managers and employees with port performance. The model was comprehensively tested using survey questionnaires. The conceptual model presented also provides a strong foundation for further research on the relationship between port resources and capabilities and port performance.

Most importantly, the theoretical foundation of this study is developed based on the RBV, which is not widely used within the context of port industry. Firms in this largely unexplored industry type are reliant on the kinds of intangible resources that may be evident in the emerging economy. An examination of key resources in a particular context would be useful in establishing the parameters and contributions of the RBV. Organizational theorists argue that, using the RBV in a new context has potential of improving the perspective as a tool and not merely reaffirming its utility. Therefore, this research contributes towards further understanding of the RBV because the unique characteristics of port industry itself are a new context that challenges some of the current notions proposed by the RBV.

5.3.3 Managerial Implication

This research finding shows that port capabilities are among the important determinants of port performance, together with organizational assets. This confirms the RBV and other port-related studies which claim that firm's capabilities is one of the major sources of firm performance and competitiveness.

Firm's capabilities are the firm's ability to sense and adapt towards the ever-changing competitive environment through the integration and continuous re-configuration of organizational skills, assets and functional competencies. Day (1994) argues that firm's capabilities will enable firms to coordinate and make productive use of their assets. Capabilities can be a source of competitive advantage if it can generate value or make a significant contribution to the perceived benefits of the end product and also imperfectly inimitable (Hamel & Prahalad, 1994; Prahalad & Hamel, 1990).

For this study, ports capabilities refer to skills and know-how of employees and managers which is based on primary and secondary activities. Primary activities of the employees and the managers are including skills in handling harbor operation, handling terminal operation, storage and yard. The secondary activities of the managers are including the skill and know-how e.g. intellectual and communication skills, strategic planning excellent management talent which are unique and valuable and organizational skills.

Capability of the employees and managers in port operation is very crucial since carriers view ships' time at ports as an expensive activity. Thus the speed of container handling and consequent vessel turnaround time are crucial issues in achieving port competitiveness (Peters, 2001). Thus, substantial productivity improvements are generally required to enable ports to meet the stringent service requirements of their customers and to obtain competitive advantages. Productivity is a measure of the efficiency of port or terminal operations, and accounts for the amount of resources usually required to perform a given task in a given time. Therefore, the level of efficiency can represent how quickly containers are handled and how quickly vessels are turned around at ports. The higher the efficiency level of a port or terminal operation, the more port users are likely to choose it as their port of call, which, in turn, will make the port gain more market shares. Port capabilities of the employees and the managers in port operation could also improve the high frequency of port calls and turnaround time (Tongzon, 1995) which, in turn, will affect the choices of shipping lines and shippers which indirectly could attract a steady and predictable performance.

In the context of the capabilities of managers in secondary activities, one of the examples is being capable to adapt new changing environments as the market environment in which ports operate has changed significantly. A successful port must constantly be capable of preparing and adopting new roles in order to cope with the changing market environment (Notteboom and Winkelmans, 2001a,b). For instance, in order to improve terminal operation performance and to integrate door-to-door transport, many shipping lines want to expand their scope to include terminal operation. If port authorities cannot realize the importance of this trend, they will lose certain competitive advantages.

Gordon et al., (2005) highlights that two key competencies are skillful workers in port operation and excellent IT experts, whereas other scholars highlight competencies such as value, quality perception and port-MIS capability (Fing-Deng 2009) and innovation capability (Yang C.C., Marlow, & Lu, 2009). These previous studies prove that port capabilities are one of major factors which help to create a sustainable competitive advantage for a port.

Employee's skills development has been a key component in driving Malaysian ports to be stay ahead from the competitors. To attain such status, ports need to upgrade its resources and develop new skills. The importance of skills in port services varies from the ability to use computerized operating systems such as expert planning systems (see above), to the ability to operate gigantic container cranes and the ability to take control of daily routine administrative tasks and responsibilities, in a timely and manner.

Recent developments in world trade and maritime industry have brought new landscapes and challenges to Malaysia's port industry. Port operators these days are exposed to dynamic phenomenon such as market changes, competitive changes, technology changes, port integration and the increase in vessel size. As a matter of fact, port success in the market place might be erased in a relatively short period of time and therefore success is not permanent due to these dynamic changes. Analyzing port's resources and capabilities is crucially important for port managers before making any strategic planning. The critical issue for ports is how they analyze all these factors and guide their organizations to consistently achieve higher performance and sustain competitive advantage. The results from this study provide a better understanding of the factors that contribute to port performance and how they relate to the issue of port resources and capabilities. Port resources should be considered as part of an entire system in the supply chain rather than in isolation, and thus port performance depends on how port can really integrate and coordinate all the resources available towards achieving higher competency and compete against other rivals.

In a practical sense, the incorporation of the RBV theory in this study will provide port managers with a better understanding on the source of the firm's competitive advantage particularly the importance of intangible resources that are capable of becoming firm's strategic assets. While resources identification is often easy once resources have been developed, managers will glean more insight into identifying resources before strategies are implemented. The RBV provides valuable framework to the managers as it enables understanding the facets of resources development and a firm's relationship to outside competition. Managers who understand and use their key resources as suggested by the RBV and thus will improve the usefulness of the RBV thus contribute to the body of strategy literature (Barney & Hesterly., 2012).

Another contribution of this research is to addressing the area of resource investment. As with any investment decision, the opportunity cost must be weighed. It is expected that the results of this research will offer some insight as to where investments may be best placed specifically with respect to investments in port resources.

The final managerial contribution of this study is that it could also serve as a guide for business managers or policy-makers in Malaysia when creating policies related to the development and competitiveness of Malaysia's port industry. More attention should be given on the importance of resources that contribute towards port performance and competitiveness.

1. Conclusion

The major goal of a business is to achieve and sustain competitiveness and thus achieve higher performance. It is a paramount task for a firm. In the context of port operators, port performance and competitiveness are very important issues since port business involves huge capital investment and at the same time has to compete head to head with other competitors either domestically or internationally. Many theories have been introduced by the scholars to explain how firms may achieve competitive advantage and one of them is the Resource-Based View theory. This theory explains that firm's competitive advantage stems from the resources that are valuable, rare, inimitable, and non-substitutable and these resources are describe as being intangible in nature. This theory argues that intangible resource is a firm's strategic resource that contributes to the performance and competitiveness of the firm. However, the RBV theory is contrary to the neo-classical economic theory that states that the strategic resource firms came from the tangible sources.

To test the notion of both theories, this research is undertaken to examine the relationship between tangible and intangible resources and port performance. Empirical research using the RBV theory such as this is rarely done, especially in the logistics and ports industry. This study found out that part of the opinion of the RBV theory can be well supported as intangible resources that port capabilities do make a larger contribution towards port performance. On the other hand, some of the intangible resources such as organizational assets and intellectual property assets do not have any impact on port performance. Lastly, this study also found that tangible resources such as financial assets, physical assets and IT assets also do not have positive relationships with port performance and this result has also been found to be contrary to what has been proved in the RBV theory. This is a new empirical contribution to the growing literature on port performance and competitiveness.

There are a few assumptions that can be made in the wake of these differences, based on studies of related literature. First, the majority of studies on firm performance and competitiveness were conducted in developed countries where the port industry is mature and consists of large size operators. In a developing country such as Malaysia, this study proves that the perspective is different, since the port industry in this country is considered as still in the growing stage. In Malaysia, the port industry began to grow after the port privatization policy was introduced in the early 1980's. This has also been influenced by the growth in import and export activities due to an increase in manufacturing activities that began in the same era. In Malaysia, there are only 8 major ports which include federal and state port operators. The limited numbers of ports might influence the results and the importance of each resource on port performance and competitiveness.

The second assumption is related to the port industry itself, which is unique when compared to other business sectors for two reasons. First, port is a business firm that is highly dependent on the locational factor in order to be a good port. Its strategic location means that the port should have good ocean depths in order to facilitate large ships. Location is also said to play an important factor for an entree-port and transshipment port because it will reduce travel costs, fuel costs, etc. The second reason is because the port industry is a business sector that requires high capital investments; it involves high expenses and high operating costs. For example, large amounts of capital were required for the purchase of cargo handling equipment such as crane and other supporting infrastructure at the harbour. Dredging cost also involves high costs and it can reach millions of dollars. Due to these reasons, tangible resources are important for the port industry in order to achieve high performance and have a competitive advantage.

As maritime sector, an essential segment of the greater transport network, Malaysian ports continue to face intense competition from other ports in the region as well as from other modes of transportation. To win the competition, they must position themselves to integrate seamlessly in the bigger picture of the transportation network. This should be achieved in a manner that meets the challenge of carrying and handling cargo in a speedy, efficient and cost-competitive manner. While they have done well to overcome the challenges posed by their competitors, there are many others looming in the horizon. There is a pressing urgency for Malaysian ports to brace for the impending competition in a further liberalized and globalized world of free trade.

It is thus crucial that Malaysian ports, at the forefront of the transport sector and trade facilitators, enhance their performance and competitiveness to improve the country's competitive advantage in an increasingly competitive global market. They need to face the challenges and realities of the environment they operate in determinedly, and overcome obstacles hindering their competitiveness decisively. It is imperative that the port regulators and operators provide more efficient and cost-competitive services, leveraging on the support and incentives already extended by the government, and through business-friendly policies such as privatization. As other ports in the region are also getting better, they will pose stiff competition to Malaysian ports in the battle for cargo and mainline operators. This calls for Malaysia to continue to train its focus on enhancing the performance and competitiveness of its ports to survive and even thrive in the face of such challenges.

References

Aaker, D. A. (1986). "Managing assets and skills: The key to sustainable competitive advantage,". *California Management Review, 31*, 91-106.

Ainuddin, R. A., Beamish, P. W., Hulland, J. S., & Rouse, M. J. (2007). Resource attributes and firm performance in international joint ventures. *Journal of World Business, 42*(1), 47-60.

Al-Bisher, H., Gray, T., & Stead, S. M. (2012). The concept of integrated national maritime policy and its application to Saudi Arabia. *Maritime Policy & Management, 39*(5), 525-541.

Alavi, M., & Leidner, D. E. (2001). Review: Knowledge management and knowledge management systems: Conceptual foundations and research issues. *MIS quarterly*, 107-136.

Ambastha, A., & Momaya, K. (2004). Competitiveness of firms: review of theory, frameworks, and models. *Singapore Management Review, 26*(1), 45-61.

Amit, R., & Schoemaker, J. P. (1993). Strategic assets and organisational rent. *Strategic Management Journal, 14*(January), 33-46.

Amit, R., & Shoemaker, P. (1993). "Strategic assets and organisational rents,". *Strategic Management Journal, 4*, 33-47.

Andersen, O., & Suat Kheam, L. (1998). Resource-based theory and international growth strategies: an exploratory study. *International Business Review, 7*(2), 163-184.

Andrew, K. R. (1971). *The concept of corporate strategy*. Homewood IL: Dow-Jones Irwin.

Armstrong, J., & Overton, T. (1977). Estimating nonresponse bias in mail surveys. *Journal of Marketing Research, 14*, 396-402.

Azevedo, S., & Ferreira, J. (2008). Competitiviness of the Port of Sines: The RBV Contribution.

Babbie, E. (2001). *The Practice of Social Research*: Wadsworth Thomson Learning, Belmont, CA.

Bain, J. (1956). Barriers to competition. *Cambridge, Massachusetts*.

Bain, J. (1959). *Industrial Organisation*. New York,NY: John Wiley & Sons.

Bain, J. (1968). *Industrial organization*. New York: John Wiley.

Bain, J. (1991). Major Characteristic of Urban waterfront redevelopment in Japan. *Marine Pollution Bulletin, 23*, 397-401.

Bang, H.-S., Kang, H.-W., Martin, J., & Woo, S.-H. (2012). The impact of operational and strategic management on liner shipping efficiency: a two-stage DEA approach. *Maritime Policy & Management, 39*(7), 653-672.

Bank, T. W. (2003). Global economic prospects, 2004. Washington: World Bank.

Barney, J. (1991). Firm resources and sustained competitive advantage. *Journal of Management, 17*(1), 99-120.

Barney, J. (1997). *Gaining and sustaining competitive advantages.*: Reading, M.A : Addison-Wesley.

Barney, J., & Hoskisson, R. E. (1990). "Strategic groups, untested assertons and research proposal". *Managerial Decision Economics, 11*, 187-198.

Barney, J., & Mackey, T. B. (2005). Testing resource-based theory.

Barros, C. P., & Athanassiou, M. (2004). Efficiency in European seaports with DEA: evidence from Greece and Portugal. *Maritime Economics & Logistics, 6*(2), 122-140.

Beach, D. P., & Alvager, K. E. (1992). *Handbook for scientific and technical research*. Englewood Cliffs, New Jersey: Prentice Hall.

Bellak, C. J., & Weiss, A. (1993). A Note on the Austrian" Diamond". *MIR: Management International Review*, 109-118.

Bernet, R. (1996). *Corporate strategy and business planning*. London: Pitman Publishing.

Blanco, B., Parez-Labajos, C., S¡nchez, L., Serrano, A., LÃ³pez, M., & Ortega, A. (2010). Innovation in spanish port sector. *Journal of Maritime Research, VII*, 71-86.

Bookbinder, J. H., & Tan, C. S. (2003). Comparison of Asian And European Logistics System. *International Journal of Physical Distribution and Logistics Management, 33*(1/2), 36-58.

Boonadir, N., Jagan, J., Muhammad, A., & Shaharuddin, A. H. (2012). Seaport Development A study on customer attracttion to West Port, Port Klang, Malaysia. *Business Management Dynamics, 1*(8), 8-19.

Bosworth, R., Libert, b. and Samek, S. (2001). "Market value, R & D and intellectual property: An empirical analysis of larger Australia firms". *The Economic Record, 77*, 323-337.

Boulton, R., Libert, B., & Samek, S. (2000). *Cracking the value code*. New York,NY: HarperCollins.

Buckley, J. P., Pass, L. C., & Prescott, K. (1988). "Measures of international competitiveness: a critical survey",. *Journal of Marketing Management, 4*(2), 175-200.

Burroughs, R. (2005). Institutional change in the Port of New York. *Maritime Policy Management,, 32*(3), 315-328.

Buzzell, R., Gale B., Sultan, R. (1975). "Market share-a key to profitability". *Harvard business review, January-February.*

Caloghirou, Y., Kastelli, I., & Tsakanikas, A. (2004). Internal capabilities and external knowledge sources: complements or substitutes for innovative performance? *Technovation, 24*(1), 29-39.

Carlton, & Perloff, J. (1994). *Modern Industrial Organization*. New York: HarperCollins College Publishers.

Carlton, W. (2004). Why barriers to entry are barriers to understanding: National Bureau of Economic Research.

Caves, R. E. (1972). *American industry:Structure, conduct, and performnace (3rd ed.)*. Ealewood Cliffs,NJ: Prentice-Hall.

Caves, R. E., & Porter, M. E. (1977). From Entry Barriers to Mobility Barriers: Conjectural Decisions and Contrived Deterrence to New Competition*. *The Quarterly Journal of Economics*, 241-261.

Chang Moon, H., Rugman, A. M., & Verbeke, A. (1995). The generalized double diamond approach to international competitiveness.

Chang Moon, H., Rugman, A. M., & Verbeke, A. (1998). A generalized double diamond approach to the global competitiveness of Korea and Singapore. *International Business Review, 7*(2), 135-150.

Cheng, T. C. E., & Choy, W. C. (2013). A study of the relationships between quality management practices and organizational performance in the shipping industry. *Maritime Economics & Logistics, 15*(1), 1-31.

Cho, D. S., & Moon, H. C. (1998). A nation's international competitiveness in different stages of economic development. *Advances in Competitiveness Research, 6*(1), 5-19.

Churchill, G. A. (1991). *Marketing Research: Methodological Foundations London*: The Dryden Press.

Clark, J., & Guy, K. (1998). Innovation and competitiveness: A review. *Technology Analysis & Strategic Management, 10*(3), 363-395.

Coakes, S. J., & Steed, L. (2007). *SPSS Version 14.0 for windows: Analysis without anguish*: John Wiley & Sons.

Coff, R. W. (1999). When competitive advantage doesn't lead to performance: The resource-based view and stakeholder bargaining power. *Organization Science, 10*(2), 119-133.

Cohen J.W. (1988). *Statistical power analysis for the behaviour sciences*. Lawrence New York: Erlbaum Associates.

Collis, D. J. (1994). "Research note: How valuable are organisational capabilities?". *Strategic Management Journal, 15 (special issue)*, 143-152.

Conner, K. (1991). An historical comparison of resource-based logic and five schools of thought within industrial organization economies: Do we have a new theory of the firm? *Journal of Management, 17*, 121-154.

Cool, K. O., & Schendel, D. (1987). Strategic group formation and performance: The case of the US pharmaceutical industry, 1963-1982. *Management science*, 1102-1124.

Council, C. C. (1992). "Building A Competitive America," *Report to the President and Congress*. US.

Creswell, J. W. (2008). *Research design: Qualitative, quantitative, and mixed methods approaches*: SAGE Publications, Incorporated.

Crisp, R. D. (1957). *Marketing Research, 3e*: Tata McGraw-Hill.

Cullinane, K., Ping, J., & Teng-Fei, W. (2005). The relationship between privatization and DEA estimates of efficiency in the container port industry. *Journal of Economics and Business, 57*(5), 433-462.

Cullinane, K., Song, D. W., Ji, P., & Wang, T. F. (2004). An application of DEA windows analysis to container port production efficiency. *Review of Network Economics, 3*(2).

Daft, R. L. (1982). *Bureaucratic versus non-bureaucratic structure and the process of innovation and change. In: Bacharach, S.B., (Ed.).* Greenwich: JAI Press.

Dai, J.-s., Xiao, H.-b., & Cui, T.-t. (2013). *Logistics Capability and Performance of Container Ports: An Empirical Research Basing on SEM.* Paper presented at the Proceedings of 2012 3rd International Asia Conference on Industrial Engineering and Management Innovation (IEMI2012).

Damanpour, F., & Gopalakrishnan, S. (2001). The dynamics of the adoption of product and process innovations in organizations. *Journal of Management Studies, 38*(1), 45-65.

Das, T. K., & Deng, B. S. (2000). "A resource-based theory of strategic alliances". *Journal of Management, 26*, 31-61.

Day, G. S. (1994). *"Capabilities for forging customer relationships"*. Paper presented at the Working Paper, Wharton Univeristy of Business, University of Pennsylvania.

De Langen, P. W., & Van Der Lugt, L. M. (2006). Governance structures of port authorities in the Netherlands. *Research in Transportation Economics, 17*(1), 109-137.

Deephouse, D. L. (2000). Media reputation as a strategic resource: An integration of mass communication and resource-based theories. *Journal of Management, 26*(6), 1091-1112.

Delener, N. (1995). *An Integrative Review of Nonresponse Errors in Survey Research : Major Influences and Strategies. In J.N. Sheth & A. Parvatiyar (eds.), Research in Marketing.* . Greenwich, Connecticut: JAI Press Inc.

Demsetz, H. (1973). Industry structure, market rivalry, and public policy. *JL & Econ., 16*, 1.

Devers, K. J., & Frankel, R. M. (2000). *Study Design in Qualitative Research-2: Sampling and Data Collection Strategies.* (Vol. 13).

Dierickx, I., & Cool, K. (1989). Asset stock accumulation and sustainability of competitive advantage. *Management Science*, 1504-1511.

Digman, L. A. (1999). *Strategic management:Concepts, processes, decisions.* Houstan,TX.: Dame Publication.

Dilman, L. A. (1978). *Mail and telephone surveys: The total design method.* New York, NY: John Wiley & Sons.

Ding, J. F. (2009a). Evaluating key capabilities and core competence for port of Keelung. *International Journal of Information and Management Sciences. v20 i2*, 269-290.

Ding, J. F. (2009b). Evaluating Key Capabilities and Core Competence for Port of Keelung. *International journal of information and management sciences, 20*(2), 269-290.

Dong-Wook, S., & Panayides, P. (2012). *Maritime Logistics: A Complete Guide to Effective Shipping and Port Management*: Kogan Page Publishers.

Ducruet, C., & Notteboom, T. (2012). The worldwide maritime network of container shipping: spatial structure and regional dynamics. *Global Networks, 12*(3), 395-423.

Edvinsson, L., & Malone, M. S. (1997). *Intellectual capital.* New York, NY: Harper Business.

Eisenhardt, K. M., Martin J.A. (2000). Dynamic capabilities:what are they? *Strategic Management Journal, 21*(10-11), 1105–1121.

Enzo, D. (2013). Good Regulations, bad regulation: a Perurian port case. *Maritime Policy & Management, 39*(6), 641-651.

Fahy, J. (2002). "A resource-based analysis of sustainabke competitive advantage in a global environment". *International Business Review, 11*, 57-78.

Feng, M., Mangan, J., & Lalwani, C. (2012). Comparing port performance: Western European versus Eastern Asian ports. *International Journal of Physical Distribution & Logistics Management, 42*(5), 490-512.

Fernandez, E., Montes, J.M., and Vazquez C.J. (2000). "Typology and strategic analysis of intangible resources: A resource-based approach,". *Technovation, 20*, 81-92.

Fiol, C. M. (2001). "Revisiting an identify-based view of sustainable competitive advantage". *Journal of Management, 21*((Special issue)), 691-699.

Frankel, E. G. (1987). *Port planning and development*: Wiley New York.

Garelli, S. (2009). IMD World Competitiveness Yearbook 2009. *Lausanne: International Institute for Management Development.*

Geralli, S. (2006). *Top Class Competitors :How nations, firms, and individuals succeed in the new world of competitiveness*: John Wiley and Sons Ltd.

Gordon, J. R. M., Lee, P. M., & Lucas, H. C. (2005). A resource-based view of competitive advantage at the Port of Singapore. *The Journal of Strategic Information Systems, 14*(1), 69-86.

Grant, R. M. (1996). Toward a knowledge-based theory of the firm. *Strategic management journal, 17*, 109-122.

Grant, R. M. (2002). *Contemporary strategy analysis (4th ed.)*. Oxford England: Blackwell Publishers.

Haezendonck, E., & Notteboom, T. (2002). *The competitive Advantage of Seaports, in : M. Huybrechts, H. Meersman E. Van de Voorde, E Van Hooydonk , A. Verbeke and W. Winkelmans (Eds)Port competitiveness: an economic and legal analysis of the factors determining the competitiveness of seaports*: Antwerp:De Boeck.

Haezendonck, E., Pison, G., Rousseeuw, P., Struyf, A., & Verbeke, A. (2000). The competitive advantage of seaport. *Maritime Economics & Logistics, 2*(2), 69-82.

Hague, P. (1993). *Questionnaire design*: Kogan Page.

Hair, J. F., Anderson, R. E., Tatham, R. L., William, C., & Blanck. (1998). Multivariate data analysis: Upper Saddle River, NJ: Prentice Hall.

Hair, J. F., Black, W. C., Babin, B. J., & Anderson, R. E. (2010). *Multivariate data analysis* Englewood Cliffs: Prentice Hall.

Hair, J. F., Tatham, R. L., Anderson, R. E., & Black, W. (2006). *Multivariate data analysis* (Vol. 6): Pearson Prentice Hall Upper Saddle River, NJ.

Hall, R. (1992). "Strategic analysis of Intangible resources". *Strategic Management Journal, 13*, 135-144.

Hamel, G., & Prahalad, C. K. (1994). *Competing for the future*. Boston M.A: Harvard Business School Press.

Hamel, G., & Prahalad, C. K. (2012). *Creating global strategic capability*. Paper presented at the Strategies in Global Competition: Selected Papers from the Prince Bertil Symposium at the Institute of International Business.

Hansen, G. S., & Wernerfelt, B. (1989). Determinants of firm performance: The relative importance of economic and organizational factors. *Strategic Management Journal, 10*(5), 399-411.

Harvey, M., Speier, C., & Novicevic, M. M. (2001). A Theory-Based Framework for Strategic Global Human Resource Staffing Policies and Practices. *International Journal of Human Resource Management, 12*, 898-915.

Hatten, K. J., & Schendel, D. E. (1977). Heterogeneity within an industry: firm conduct in the US brewing industry, 1952-71. *The Journal of Industrial Economics, 26*(2), 97-113.

Hawawini, G., Subramanian, V., & Verdin, P. (2003). "Is Performance Driven by Industry- or Firm-Specific Factors?: A New Look at the Evidence,". *Strategic Management Journal 24*

Hayes, R. H., & Abernathy, W. J. (1980). Managing Our Way to Economic Decline. *Harvard Business Review, 58*, 67-77.

Haynes, K. E. (1997). Labor markets and regional transportation improvements: the case of high-speed trains An introduction and review. *The Annals of Regional Science, 31*(1), 57-76.

Heaver, T., Meersman, H., & Van de Voorde, E. (2001). Co-operation and competition in international container transport: strategies for ports. *Maritime Policy & Management, 28*(3), 293-305.

Hellofs, L. L., & Jacobson, R. (1999). Market share and customers' perceptions of quality: when can firms grow their way to higher versus lower quality? *The Journal of Marketing*, 16-25.

Henderson, B. D. (1979). *Henderson on Corporate Strategy*: Mentor, New York.

Hitts, M. A., Keats, B. W., & DeMarie, S. M. (1998). Navigating in the new competitive landscape: Building strategic flexibility and competitive advantage in the 21st century. *Acedemic of Management Executive, 12*(4).

Hodgetts, R. M. (1993). Porter's diamond framework in a Mexican context. *MIR: Management International Review*, 41-54.

Hoskisson, R. E., Hitt, M. A., Wan, W. P., & Yiu, D. (1999). Theory and research in strategic management: Swings of a pendulum. *Journal of Management, 25*(3), 417-456.

Hout, T. M., Porter, M. E., & Rudden, E. (1982). *How global companies win out*: Graduate School of Business Administration, Harvard University.

Hoyle, B. (1999). Port Concerntration, inter-port competition and revitalization:the case of Mombasa, Kenya. *Maritime Policy and Management, 26*(2), 161-174.

Hunt, M. (1972). *"Competition in the Major Home Appliance Industry"*. Harvard University.

Huselid, M. A. (1995). The impact of human resource management practices on turnover, productivity, and corporate financial performance. *Academy of management journal*, 635-672.

Huybrechts, M., Meersman, H., Van de Voorde, E., Van Hooydowk, E., Verbeke, A., & Winkelmans, W. (2002). *Port Competitiveness*. Antwerp: DeBoeck.

Hwang, C. C., & Chiang, C. H. (2010). Cooperation and Competitiveness of Intra-Regional Container Ports. *Journal of the Eastern Asia Society for Transportation Studies, 8*, 2283-2298.

Ircha, M. (2001). Serving tomorrow's mega-size containerships: Canadian solution. *International Journal of Maritime Economics, 3*(3), 318-332.

Itami, H., Roehl T. W. (1987). *Mobilizing invisible assets*. Cambrigde, MA: Harvard University Press.

Jacobson, R. (1987). 'The validity of ROI as a measure of business performance'. *American Economic Review, 77*(3), 470-478.

Jacobson, R. (1992). The" Austrian" school of strategy. *Academy of management review*, 782-807.

Jacobson, R., & Aaker, D. A. (1985). "Is market share all that it's cracked up to be?". *Journal of Marketing, 57*, 53-70.

Kay, J. (1988). *"The R and D Function:Corporate strategy and structure," In G. Dosi, C. Freeman, R. Nelson, G. Silverberg, and L. Soete (Eds.), Technical Change and Economic Theory*. New York, NY: Printer Publishers.

Khatri, N., & Ng, H. A. (2000). The role of intuition in strategic decision making. *Human Relations, 53*(1), 57-86.

Kim, W. C., & Mauborgne, R. (2005). Blue ocean strategy. *Harvard Business School Press, Boston, MA*.

King, A. W., & Zeithaml, C. P. (2001). Competencies and firm performance: examining the causal ambiguity paradox. *Strategic Management Journal, 22*(1), 75-99.

Kogut, B. (2000). "The network as knowledge: Generative rules and the emergence of structure,". *Strategic Management Journal, 21*, 405-425.

Kogut, B., & Zander, U. (1996). "What do firms do?". *Organization Science, 7*, 502-518.

Kotler, P. (1994). *Marketing Management: Analysis, Planning, Implementation, and Control. 8th ed.* Englewood Cliffs, NJ: Prentice Hall.

Krugman, P. (1994). Competitiveness: a dangerous obsession. *Foreign affairs*, 28-44.

Krugman., P. R., & Obstfeld, M. (2003). *International Economics: Theory and Policy, 4th Edition*.: New York: Harper Collins.

Lam, J. S. L., & Yap, W. Y. (2006). A measurement and comparison of cost competitiveness of container ports in Southeast Asia. *Transportation, 33*(6), 641-654.

Langen, P. (2002). Clustering and performance: the case of maritime clustering in The Netherlands. *Maritime Policy & Management, 29*(3), 209-221.

Langen, P. (2004). Governance in seaport clusters. *Maritime Economics & Logistics, 6*(2), 141-156.

Langen, P., & Pallis, A. A. (2007). Entry barriers in seaports. *Maritime Policy & Management, 34*(5), 427-440.

Lazear, E. (2000). "Performance pay and productivity". *American Economic Review, 90*, 1346-1361.

Learned, E. P., Christiensen, C. R., Andrew, K. R., & Guth, W. D. (1969). *Business Policy: Text and Cases (rev. ed.)*. Homewood IL: Richard D. Irwin.

Lee-Partridge, J. E., Teo, T. S. H., & Lim, V. K. G. (2000). Information technology management: the case of the Port of Singapore Authority. *The Journal of Strategic Information Systems, 9*(1), 85-99.

Lee, T., & Wilde, L. L. (1980). Market structure and innovation: a reformulation. *The Quarterly Journal of Economics, 94*(2), 429-436.

Leontif, W. W. (1953). *Domestic Production and Foreign Trade*. Paper presented at the Proceeding of American Philosophical Society.

Levitas, E., & Chi, T. (2002). Rethinking Rouse and Daellenbach's rethinking: Isolating vs. testing for sources of sustainable competitive advantage. *Strategic Management Journal, 23*(10), 957-962.

Levitt, T. (1993). The globalization of markets. *Readings in international business: a decision approach, 249*.

Lipczynski, J., Wilson, J. O. S., & Goddard, J. B. (2005). *Industrial organization: competition, strategy, policy*: Financial Times/Prentice Hall.

Lirn, T., Thanopoulou, H., Beynon, M., & Beresford, A. (2004). An application of AHP on transhipment port selection: a global perspective. *Maritime Economics & Logistics, 6*(1), 70-91.

Low, J. M., & Tang, L. C. (2012). Network effects in the East Asia container ports industry. *Maritime Policy & Management, 39*(4), 369-386.

Lun, H. H. V., Lai, K. H., & Cheng, T. C. E. (2009). Intermodal transport capability. *Shipping Transport Logistics, 1*(17-33).

Luo, W., Van Hoek, R. I., & Roos, H. H. (2001). Cross-cultural logistics research: a literature review and propositions. *International Journal of Logistics, 4*(1), 57-78.

Maersk, L. (2011). Maersk Line contracts additional 10 Triple-E vessels. *Maersk Line, June, 27*, 2011. Retrieved from

Magala, M. (2004). *Opportunity Capture and Growth Strategies for Regional Ports: A Modelling Approach*. Degree Of Doctor Philosophy, Victoria University, Victoria.

Magala, M., & Sammons, A. (2008). A new approach to port choice modelling. *Maritime Economics & Logistics, 10*(1), 9-34.

Mahoney, J., & Pandian, J. R. (1992). The resource-based view within the conversation of strategic management. *Strategic Management Journal, 13*(5), 363–380.

Malchow, M., & Kanafani, A. (2001). A disaggregate analysis of factors influencing port selection. *Maritime Policy & Management, 28*(3), 265-277.

Martin, L., Westgren, R., & van Duren, E. (1991). Agribusiness competitiveness across national boundaries. *American Journal of Agricultural Economics, 73*(5), 1456-1464.

Mason, E. S. (1939). Price and production policies of large-scale enterprise. *The American Economic Review*, 61-74.

Mathews, J. A. (2006). Dragon Multinationals: New Players in 21st Century Globalization. *Asia Pacific Journal of Management, 23*, 5-27.

Mauri, A. J., & Michaels, M. P. (1998). Firm and industry effects within strategic management: an empirical examination. *Strategic Management Journal, 19*(3), 211-219.

Mc Kinnon, A. (2011). *Hong Kong and Shenzhen Ports: Challenges, Opportunities and Global Competitiveness*.

McGahan, & Anita, M. (1999a). The performance of U.S. corporations: 1981-1994. *Journal of Industrial Economics, 67*(4).

McGahan, Anita, M., & Porter, M. E. (1997). How much does industry matter, really? *Strategic Management Journal, 18*(Summer Special Issue), 15-30.

Michalisin, Smith, R. D., & Kline, D. M. (1997). In search of strategic assets. *International Journal of Organizational Analysis, 5*, 360-387.

Miller, J. W. (2009). "The Mega Containers Invade",. *Wall Street Journal*.

Mintzberg, H. (1993). *Structure in fives: Designing effective organizations*: Prentice-Hall, Inc.

Mintzberg, H., Ahlstrand, B., & Lampel, J. (1998). *Strategy Safari: A Guided Tour through the Wilds of Strategic Management*. New York: The Free Press.

Morgan, R. M., & Hunt, S. D. (1994). The commitment-trust theory of relationship marketing. *The Journal of Marketing*, 20-38.

Murphy, P. R., Dalenberg, D. R., & Daley, J. M. (1991). Analyzing international water transportation: the perspectives of large US industrial corporations. *Journal of Business Logistics, 12*(1), 169-190.

Murths. (1998). "Country Capabilities and the Strategic State: How National Political Institutions Affect MNC Strategies",. *Strategic Management Journal, 15*, 113-129.

Musso, E., Ferrari, C., & Benacchio, M. (2001). *Co-operation in maritime and port industry and its effects on market structure,*. Paper presented at the WCTR Conference, Seoul.

Nahapiet, J., & Ghoshal, S. (1998). Social capital, intellectual capital, and the organizational advantage. *Academy of Management Review*, 242-266.

Nelson, R. R., & Winter, S. G. (1982). *An evolutionary theory of economic change*: Belknap press.

Newbert, S. L. (2007). Empirical research on the resourceâ€?based view of the firm: an assessment and suggestions for future research. *Strategic Management Journal, 28*(2), 121-146.

Nik Azli, M., Jagan, J., Roszita, M. S., Nik Muhammad Aslaam, & Saharuddin, A. H. (2011). *A study on competitiveness of rivalry and technology services in port development.* Paper presented at the 2nd International Conference on Business and Economic Research (2nd ICBER 2011) Proceeding, Malaysia.

Nonaka, I., & Takeuchi, H. (1995). *The knowledge-creating company: How Japanese companies create the dynamics of innovation*: Oxford University Press, USA.

Notteboom, & Winkelmans. (2001). 'Structural changes in logistics: how will port authorities face the challenge? *Maritime Policy and Management, 28*(1), pp. 71-89.

Notteboom, T. (2004). Container shipping and ports: an overview. *Review of Network Economics, 3(2)*(86-106).

Notteboom, T., Pallis, A. A., & Farrell, S. (2012). Terminal concessions in seaports revisited. *Maritime Policy & Management, 39*(1), 1-5.

Notteboom, T., & Rodrique, J. P. (2011). Global container terminal operators: from diversification to rationalization?

Notteboom, T., & Winkelmans. (2001). Structural changes in logistics: how will port authorities face the challenge? *Maritime Policy & Management, 28*(1), 71-89.

Nunnally, J. C. (1978). *Psychometric Theory*: McGraw-Hill Book, New York.

Ohmae, K. (1985). Managing innovation and new products in key Japanese industries. *Research Management, 28*(4), 11-18.

Olivier, D. (2005). Private Entry and emerging partnerships in the container terminal industry: evidence from Asia. *Maritime Economics and Logistics, 7*(2), 87-115.

Olivier, D., Parola, F., Slack, B., & Wang, J. J. (2007). The Time Scale of Internationalisation: The Case of the Container Port Industry. *Maritime Economics and Logistics, 9*(1), 1-34.

Pagano, A. M., Wang, G. W., Sanchez, O. V., & Ungo, R. (2013). Impact of privatization on port efficiency and effectiveness: results from Panama and US ports. *Maritime Policy & Management, 40*(2), 100-115.

Pallant, J. (2001). *SPSS Survival Manual.* : Open University Press, Buckingham and Philadephia. .

Pallis, A. A., Notteboom, T., & Langen, P. (2008). Concession agreements and market entry in the container terminal industry. *Maritime Economics & Logistics, 10*(3), 209-228.

Pallis, A. A., Vitsounis, T. K., & De Langen, P. W. (2010). Port economics, policy and management: Review of an emerging research field. *Transport Reviews, 30*(1), 115-161.

Panayides, P. M. (2006). Maritime logistics and global supply chains: towards a research agenda. *Maritime Economics & Logistics, 8*(1), 3-18.

Parola, F., Satta, G., & Caschili, S. (2013). Unveiling co-operative networks and 'hidden families' in the container port industry. *Maritime Policy & Management*(ahead-of-print), 1-21.

Penrose, E. (1959a). *The Theory of the Growth of the Firm.* Oxford.: Oxford University Press.

Peteraf, M. A. (1993). The cornerstones of competitive advantage: a resourceâ€?based view. *Strategic Management Journal, 14*(3), 179-191.

Peters, H. J. (2001). Developments in global seatrade and container shipping markets: their effects of the port industry
and private sector involvement. *International Journal of Maritime Economics, 3*, 3-26.

Peterson, J., & Barras, R. (1987). Measuring international competitiveness in services. *Service Industries Journal, 7*(2), 131-142.

Phillips, L. W. (1981). "Assessing measurement error in key informant report: A methodological note on organizational analysis in marketing,". *Journal of Marketing Research, 18*, 395-415.

Photis, M. P., & Gray, R. (1999). An empirical assessment of relational competitive advantage in professional ship management. *Maritime Policy & Management, 26*(2), 111-125.

Pillai, J. S. (2006). ANU-Digital Collections: Service exports from a small city-state: the case of Port of Singapore Authority

Pinder, D., & Slack, B. (2004). *Shipping and ports in the twenty-first century: globalisation, technological change and the environment* (Vol. 6): Psychology Press.

Porter, M. E. (1980). *Competitive Strategy*. New York, NY: The Free Press.

Porter,M. E. (1985). Competitive advantage: Creating and sustaining superior performance: Free Press New York.

Porter, M. E. (1990). *The competitive advantage of nations: with a new introduction*: Free Press.

Porter, M. E. (1990a). *The Competitive Advantage of Nations*. New York: Free Press, MacMillan.

Porter, M. E. (2008). On Competition, updated and expanded edition. *Harvard Business School Press, Boston.*

Porter, M. E., Sachs, J., Cornelius, P. K., McArthur, J. W., Forum, W. E., & Development, H. U. C. f. I. (2002). *Global Competitiveness Report, 2001-2002*: Oxford university press.

Powell, W. W., Koput, K. W., & Smith-Doerr, L. (1996). Interorganizational collaboration and the locus of innovation: Networks of learning in biotechnology. *Administrative Science Quarterly*, 116-145.

Prahalad, C. K., & Hamel, G. (1990). The core competence of the corporation. *Harvard Business Review, 68*(3), 79-91.

Punch, K. F. (2003). *Survey research: The basics*: SAGE Publications Limited.

Reed, R., & DeFillippi, R. J. (1990). Causal ambiguity, barriers to imitation, and sustainable competitive advantage. *Academy of Management Review*, 88-102.

Rogers, D. M. A. (1996). "Knowldege management gains momentum in industry,". *Research-Technology Management, 39*, 5-7.

Roll, Y., & Hayuth, Y. (1993). Port performance comparison applying data envelopment analysis (DEA). *Maritime Policy and Management, 20*(2), 153-161.

Roquebert, J. A., Phillips, R. L., & Westfall, P. A. (1996). Market Vs Management:What 'Drives Profitability? *Strategic Management Journal, 17*(8), 653-664.

Rousseau, D. (1985). *"Issues of level in organisatinal research:Multi-level and cross-level perspectives," In L.L Cumming and b. M Shaw (Eds.).* Greenwich, C.T: JAI Press.

Rozenblat, C. (2004). Les villes portuaires en Europe, analyse comparative. *CNRS, Montpellier.*

Rubin, P. H. (1973). The expansion of firms. *Journal of Political Economy, 81*, 936–949.

Rugman, A. M., & Verbeke, A. (2002). Edith Penrose's contribution to the Resource-Based View of strategic management. *Strategic Management Journal, 23*(8), 769-780.

Rumelt, R. P. (1974). *Strategy, Structure, and Economic Performance*. Boston: Harvard University Press.

Rumelt, R. P. (1984). *"Towards a strategic theory of the firm" In R.B lamb (Ed.) Competitive Strategic Management*. Englewood Cliffs, NJ: Prentice-Hall.

Rumelt, R. P. (1991). 'How much does industry matter?'. *Strategic Management Journal, 12*(3), 167-185.

Rumelt, R. P., & Teece, D. J. (1994). *Fundamental issues in strategy: A research agenda*: Harvard Business Press.

Rupa, D. (2013). Kuantan Port expansion to boost trade. 1-2. Retrieved from http://www.btimes.com.my/Current_News/BTIMES/articles/kn26/kn26.pdf

Sakakibara, M., & Porter, M. E. (2001). Competing at home to win abroad: evidence from Japanese industry. *Review of Economics and Statistics, 83*(2), 310-322.

Saunders, M., Lewis, P., & Thornhill, A. (2009). Research Methods for business students 4th edition Pearson education limited.

Scherer, F. M. (1980). *Industrial market structure and economic performance (2nd Ed)*. Chicago IL: Ran McNally.

Schøyen, H., & Odeck, J. (2013). The technical efficiency of Norwegian container ports: A comparison to some Nordic and UK container ports using Data Envelopment Analysis (DEA). *Maritime Economics & Logistics, 15*(2), 197-221.

Schroeder, R. G., Bates, K. A., & Junttila, M. A. (2002). "A resource-based view of manufacturing and the relationship to manufacturing performnace,". *Strategic Management Journal, 23*, 105-117.

Schumpeter, J. (1934). *The theory of economic development*. Cambridge, Mass: Harvard University Press,.

Schumpeter, J. (1942). *Capitalism, Socialism, and Democracy*. New York: Harper & Row.

Schumpeter, J. (1950). *Capitalism, Socialism, and Democracy*. New York: Harper & Row.

Scott, B. R., & Lodge, G. C. (1985). US competitiveness in the world economy. *The International Executive, 27*(1), 26-26.

Sekaran, & Bougie, R. (2010). Research methods for business: A skill building approach. Wiley: London.

Short, D. G. (1993). *Fundamentals of Financial Accounting (7th ed.)*. Homewood,IL: Richard D. Irwin.

Sihombing, L. (2007). *The Improvement of Nation Invesment Competitiveness: Financial Innovation for Seaport Infrastructure Financing*. Paper presented at the International Conference on Port, Coastal and Ocean Engineering, Institute of Technology Bandung (ITB), Bandung, Indonesia, 2007.

Sirmon, D. G., Hitt, M. A., & Ireland, R. D. (2007). Managing firm resources in dynamic environments to create value: Looking inside the black box. *Academy of management review, 32*(1), 273-292.

Slater, S. F. (1997). "Developing a customer value-based theory of a firm,". *Journal of the Academy of Marketing Science, 25*, 162-167.

Smith, P. A. C., Saint-Onge, H. (1996). The evolutionary organization: avoiding a fate. *Learning Organization, The, 3*(4), 4-21.

Solow, R. M. (1957). Technical Change and the Aggregate Production Function.". *Review of Economics and Statistics, 39*(3), 312-320.

Song, D. W., & Yeo, K. T. (2004). A competitive analysis of Chinese container ports using the analytic hierarchy process. *Maritime Economics & Logistics, 6*(1), 34-52.

Soo, C. W. M., D.F., and Devinney, T.M. (2001). *"The Process of Knowledge Creation in Organizations"*. Paper presented at the Working Paper, Australian Graduate School of Management, New South Wales, Australia.

Spanos, Y. E., & Lioukas, S. (2001). An examination into the causal logic of rent generation: contrasting Porter's competitive strategy framework and the resources-based perspective. *Strategic Management Journal, 22*(10), 907-934.

Spender, J.-C., & Grant, R. M. (1996). Knowledge and the firm: overview. *Strategic Management Journal, 17*, 5-9.

Starr, J. T. (1994). The mid-Atlantic load centre: Baltimore or Hampton Roads? *Maritime Policy and Management, 21*(3), 219-227.

Stigler, G. J. (1961). The economics of information. *The Journal of Political Economy, 69*(3), 213-225.

Stigler, G. J. (1966). *The theory of price*. New York: Macmillan.

Stopford, M., & Badenfuller, W. F. (1994). Creating Corporate Enterpreneurship. *Strategic Management Journal, 12*(7), 521-536.

Talley, W. K. (2009). *Port economics*: Taylor & Francis.

Tang, L. C., Low, J. M., & Lam, S. W. (2011). Understanding port choice behavior—a network perspective. *Networks and Spatial Economics, 11*(1), 65-82.

Teece, D. J. (1988). Capturing value from technological innovation: Integration, strategic partnering, and licensing decisions. *Interfaces*, 46-61.

Teece, D. J. (2000). Strategies for managing knowledge assets: the role of firm structure and industrial context. *Long range planning, 33*(1), 35-54.

Teece, D. J., & Shuen, P. A. (1997). Dynamic capabilities and strategic management. *Strategic Management Journal, 18*(7), 509–533.

Tongzon, J., & Heng, W. (2005). Port privatization, efficiency and competitiveness: Some empirical evidence from container ports (terminals). *Transportation Research Part A: Policy and Practice, 39*(5), 405-424.

UNCTAD. (1992). Strategic Planning for Port Authorities: United Nations, Geneva.

UNCTAD. (2012). Review of Maritime Transport 2012. Retrieved from http://unctad.org/en/PublicationsLibrary/rmt2012_en.pdf

Utterback, J. M., & Abernathy, W. J. (1975). A dynamic model of process and product innovation. *Omega, 3*(6), 639-656.

Van de Voorde, E. (2005). *What future the maritime sector? Some considerations on globalisation,co-operation and market power, in: Kanafani, Adib and Katsuhiko Kuroda (Eds) Global Competition in Transportation Markets: Analysis and Policy Making.* Amsterdam, The Netherlands: Elsevier JAI.

Van de Voorde, E., & Vanelslander, T. (2009). *Market power and vertical and horizontal integration in the maritime shipping and port industry*: OECD/ITF.

Vause, B. (2009). *Guide to analysing companies* (Vol. 44): Bloomberg Press.

Vincent, F. V., & Hassiba, B. (2013). Maritime transports and international seaborne trade. *Maritime Policy & Management, 40*(3), 226-242.

Wang, G. W., Knox, K. J., & Lee, P. T.-W. (2013). A study of relative efficiency between privatised and publicly operated US ports. *Maritime Policy & Management, 40*(4), 351-366.

Welbourne, T. M., & Wright, P. M. (1997). *"Which resources matter in initial public offering firms? A longitudinal comparison of five resources' contributions to firm performance",.*

Wernerfelt, B. (1984). A resource-based view of the firm. *Strategic Management Journal, 5*(2), 171–180.

Wiegmans, B. W., Hoest, A. V. D., & Notteboom, T. E. (2008). Port and terminal selection by deep-sea container operators. *Maritime Policy & Management, 35*(6), 517-534.

Wiggins, R. R., & Ruefli, T. W. (1995). Necessary conditions for the predictive validity of strategic groups: Analysis without reliance on clustering techniques. *Academy of Management Journal*, 1635-1656.

William, J. A. (1992). "How sustainable is your competitive advantage?". *California Management Review, 34*, 29-51.

Winter, S. (1995). 'Four R's of profitability: Rents, resources, routines, and replication. In C. A. Montgomery (Ed.), *Resources in an Evolutionary Perspective: A Synthesis of Evolutionary and Resource-based Approaches to Strategy.* Norwell, MA and Dordrecht.: Kluwer Academic.

World Bank. (2001). Port Reform Tool Kit Retrieved 23/4/2009, 2009, from http://www.worldbank.org/transport/ports/toolkit.htm

Woudsma, C., Hall, P., & O'Brien, T. (2009). Innovation and stakeholder collaboration in west coast gateways: An analysis of the seaport and freight movement industries. *Report. Vancouver: The Asia Pacific Foundation of Canada.*

Yamin, S., Mavondo, F., Gunasekaran, A., & Sarros, J. C. (1997). A study of competitive strategy, organisational innovation and organisational performance among Australian manufacturing companies. *International Journal of Production Economics, 52*(1), 161-172.

Yanbing, Y., Zhongzhen, Y., Zan, Y., & Zhi, Z. (2005). *Evaluation of competition ability and market share for conteiner port.* Paper presented at the Eastern Asia Society for Transportation Studies.

Yang C.C., Marlow, P. B., & Lu, C. S. (2009). Assessing resources, logistics service capabilities, innovation capabilities and the performance of container shipping services in Taiwan. *International Journal of Production Economics, 122*(1), 4-20.

Yang, X., Low, J. M. W., & Tang, L. C. (2011). Maritime Trade Evolutions and Port City Developments in Asia. *Advances in Maritme Logistics and Supply Chain System* Retrieved 12th December 2011, 2011

Yap, W. Y., & Lam, J. S. L. (2006a). An interpretation of inter-container port relationships from the demand perspective. *Maritime Policy & Management, 31*, 337-355.

Yeo, G. T., Roe, M., & Dinwoodie, J. (2008). Evaluating the competitiveness of container ports in Korea and China. *Transportation Research Part A: Policy and Practice, 42*(6), 910-921.

Yin, R. K. (2002). *Case study research: Design and methods* (Vol. 5): SAGE Publications, Incorporated.

Zhu, K., & Kraemer, K. L. (2002). E-commerce metrics for net-enhanced organizations: Assessing the value of e-commerce to firm performance in the manufacturing sector. *Information Systems Research, 13*(3), 275-295.

Zikmund, W. G. (1991). *Business Research Methods,* : Chicago: Dryden. .

Zollo, M., & Winter, S. (1999). *"From organisational routines to dynamic capabilities,".* Paper presented at the Working Paper 99-07, Regined H.Jones Center, The Wharton School, University of Pennsylvania.

9 798889 590958

Printed by Libri Plureos GmbH in Hamburg,
Germany